ALOW□
S & CRAFTS HOME

·BUNGALOW·

THE ULTIMATE ARTS & CRAFTS HOME

·BUNGALOW·

THE ULTIMATE ARTS & CRAFTS HOME

JANE POWELL & LINDA SVENDSEN

Gibbs Smith, Publisher
Salt Lake City

THIS BOOK IS DEDICATED TO MY FRIEND JEANNETTE SHERWIN (1948-2004), GIRL ROCK-THROWER, FOUNDER OF THE EAST BAY LADIES CITY HALL JOURNALISM AND TWIG-GILDING SOCIETY, AND MY BIGGEST FAN, WHOSE ONLY FAILING WAS THAT SHE DIDN'T LIKE PUNS. IN HER HONOR, THERE ISN'T A SINGLE PUN IN THIS BOOK.

First Edition

08 07 06 05 04   5 4 3 2 1

Text © 2004 Jane Powell

Photographs © 2004 Linda Svendsen

Published by

Gibbs Smith, Publisher

P.O. Box 667

Layton, Utah 84041

Orders: 1.800.748.5439

www.gibbs-smith.com

Designed by Dawn DeVries Sokol

Printed and bound in Hong Kong

Library of Congress Control Number: 2004108298

ISBN 1-58685-304-X

□ACKNOWLEDGMENTS□

Although I am alone when I sit in front of the computer trying to think of something new to say about Arts and Crafts, a book such as this is always a collaborative effort. I must first thank Linda Svendsen for her always fabulous photography, without which my words would not convey very much, and my editor, Suzanne Taylor, for making sure the words make sense. If I had known how much clerical work was involved in writing a book, I might never have taken it up—keeping track of photos, addresses, names and phone numbers is not my strong suit, so I apologize right now to anyone I have inadvertently left out, and I am sure there are quite a few. I also apologize if I have placed a house in a different city from where it is actually located—nationwide similarities in bungalows, combined with bad note-taking on my part, and the fact that there were a total of eleven hundred photos probably means I messed up on quite a few of them. We would never have found houses to photograph without referrals from many people, including John Atkin and Jo Scott-B in Vancouver, British Columbia; Steve Austin and Cathy Hitchcock of Austin-Hitchcock Restorations in Portland, Oregon; Jennifer Barr of the Victoria Heritage Foundation in Victoria, British Columbia; Steve Ciancio, Robert Rust and Pam McCreary in Denver; Tim Counts of the Twin Cities Bungalow Club in Minneapolis; Kathy Couturie in southern California; Laurie Crogan, Adam Janeiro of the West Adams Heritage Association, and Suzanne Houchin in Los Angeles; Allison Freedland of the Historic Chicago Bungalow Association in Chicago; Carlen Hatala of the City of Milwaukee and Denise Hice of Historic Milwaukee in Milwaukee; John Hopkins and Marsha Oates, and Sue Williams in Memphis; Bob Kneisel of the Bungalow Heaven Neighborhood Association in Pasadena; Larry Kreisman of Historic Seattle, Clint Miller, and Laurie Taylor in Seattle; Suzanne and Dennis Prieur in Eagle Rock; John Ribovich in Pleasanton; and Cynthia Thompson of the Pierpont Inn in Ventura.

We are grateful to the many homeowners who graciously opened their bungalows to us, making this book possible, including: Rob Bruce and Greg Gill in Altadena; Lynne and Audel Davis, Jean and Roger Moss, Don and Arlyce Feist, Homayoon Kazerooni and Audrey Shoji, Jeanne Franken and Fred Harder, Richard Pettler and Wanda Westberg, Linda McCain and Mark Novakowski, Janet Mark and Terry Geiser in Berkeley; Marty and Ron Thomas, Lisa Klein, Linda and Mark Anderson, Jim and Margaret de Lauria, Nancy Jane Lauren and Frank Pokorny in Chicago; Christopher and Wendy Crosby, Sandy Mazarakis and Neil Burris, and Charlene Sloan in Denver; Suzanne and Dennis Prieur in Eagle Rock; Marty May in Florida; Leonard Fenton, Evan Geisler in Hollywood; Ellen and David Dobin in Lafayette; Rip and Nicole Haney, Genevieve Posey, Michael and Melinda Wayt, Janey Outlan, Edith and Bob Heller, Marsha Hayes, Linda Oxford and Jim Rice, Carol Raiford, John and Meridith Starling, Sean and Jitka McGivney, Davey and M.J. Weakes, Sam and Charlotte Cantor, Erin Berg, and Mari Askew in Memphis; Steve and Cathy Hoelter, Keith and Denise Hice, Kurt and Rachel Young-Binter, Deanne Ohman and Al Jacobi, Mark and LeeAnn Knippel in Milwaukee; Julie Hardgrove and Cliff Cline, Ann and Ken Katz in Oakland; Will Castagna in Ojai; Ann and Andre Chaves, Arno Grether, Kristopher Doe and Susan Halpin in Pasadena; John Ribovich and Lisa Alba in Pleasanton; Steve Austin and Cathy Hitchcock, Robert and Melissa Hogan in Portland; Robert Noble, Richard Reutlinger in San Francisco; Thomas Stangeland, Olivia Dresher, Larry Willits, Carrie Schnelker and Michael Sobiek, Pamela and Gerard Zytnicki, Barbara Griffin and Judy Cherin, Mary Fields and John Aylward, Bob Welland and Mary Casey, Mary-Alice Pomputius and Walter Smith, Jessie Jones and Matt Johnson, Shelley and Michael O'Clair, Brian Coleman and Howard Cohen in Seattle; Kathy and Bill Couturie in a southern California town that shall remain nameless; Geoff Corso and Marshall McClintock in Tacoma; Heather and Bill Andrews in Vancouver, British Columbia; Celia Orozco, Bill Gould, Jean Gould Bryant in Ventura; Suzanne and Patrick Bulmer, Paul and Marilynne Convey, Judith and Richard Andersen, Sheila and Jim Colwill in Victoria, British Columbia.

As always, I want to thank my father, Nelson Powell, my sisters, Nancy Klapak and Mary Enderle, and my cats, Milo, Zoe, and especially Ubu, who is content to lie quietly in my lap while I type. And I want to thank whatever cosmic forces brought me to the Sunset House, which is a daily source of beauty, joy, and amazement.

—Jane Powell

◻ CONTENTS ◻

Architect Julia Morgan designed this home for a tree-studded Berkeley, California hillside in 1905. The soaring space of its redwood-paneled living room is anchored by a clinker brick fireplace, flanked on one side by a built-in bookcase and on the other by large casement windows. To the right, French doors open into the dining room, and the stair landing to the right of the dining room doors is anchored by a shallow niche with shelving for display. On the other side of the living room, doors lead to an enclosed porch. In the foreground, a lamp by contemporary craftsman Michael Ashford sits on a three-drawer Gustav Stickley library table with a Stickley Brothers cane seated chair. In front of the table, seating is provided by a Gustav Stickley settle. A cube chair by the fireplace is flanked by a Limbert tea table with another Michael Ashford lamp, while under the windows, a Stickley Brothers hall settle is adorned with modern-day embroidered pillows by Dianne Ayres. As is typical in bungalows, the front door opens directly into this room.

□ FOREWORD □

SERIOUSNESS IS THE ONLY
REFUGE OF THE SHALLOW.

O S C A R   W I L D E

With the recent plethora of bungalow books on the market, one has
to ask if there is need for another. Well of course there is! Otherwise I
would be happily spending my time rebuilding windows and painting or
restoring the kitchen here at the fabulous Sunset House, instead of sitting
at the computer racking my tiny brain trying to find the words to explain
about bungalows and why they are so fabulous that I would devote my
life to them. I do love them all—tiny, big, zany, architecturally restrained,
run-down, restored, designed by architects, built from plan books,
ready-cut, brick, wood, stone, stucco—every one of them appeals to me
on some level. I love seeing how they differ from city to city, and even
neighborhood to neighborhood, yet remain true to their roots despite
allowing for endless variation. I occasionally despair that there are so
many people who don't appreciate them, and I also bemoan the new
tacked-on "Craftsman style" going up on tract houses in the suburbs
(just for your information, homebuilders, three knee-braces in a gable
and a column made of "cultured stone" do not a bungalow make,
especially not one whose front facade consists mainly of a garage door).

We considered many facetious names for this book—*Bungalows
24/7, All Bungalows All the Time, Bungalows: The Sequel, The Bungalow*

That it is possible to build a new bungalow and do it right is clearly shown by this brand-new house in Lafayette, California. Though it does have three knee braces in the gable, the attention to proportion and details such as the gable vent and window, the porch pergola, window muntins, and porch railing, make it nearly indistinguishable from a vintage bungalow.

Strikes Back, Silence of the Bungalows—I think you get the idea. This book is hardly the last word on bungalows; the surface has barely been scratched. Nonetheless, we have

managed to find photos of never-before-published bungalows to show (with a couple of exceptions). However, we cheated a little bit—a couple of houses are actually two stories and don't technically qualify, but we just couldn't pass them up. Unlike many books of this type, the pictures are not arranged house by house; rather, they have been split up into individual rooms or features. There are several reasons for this. Some houses had only a few rooms that the owner would allow us to photograph, or that would photograph well. (Some rooms, frankly, are not very interesting in a photograph although they may be perfectly fine in real life.) Plus,

ABOVE: Chicago and the Midwest aren't the only places where the influences of Prairie School architecture are found. This Prairie-style bungalow in Memphis, designed by an architect who had worked for Frank Lloyd Wright, takes the overhanging eaves of the style to extremes, while still using the limestone pillars that are typical of Memphis bungalows.

LEFT: The Sunset House was designed and built in 1905 by Jesse Matteson, who also happened to own a local lumber company, which probably explains his use of massive old-growth Douglas fir timbers throughout his home. After all, he was getting them wholesale. The unusual paneling, a twist on the more common board-and-batten, features boards that have been chamfered (cut at an angle) along each edge, creating a V groove where two boards meet. A one-inch square molding is set on edge in each groove, forming a triangular profile. Below the two-by-eight horizontal bands, the triangular moldings are interrupted every few inches by chamfered blocks, numbering forty-five in the entry hall alone. Above, eight-inch-square timbers support the second floor, while the ceiling between them is paneled with board-and-batten. A post light with a ribbed shade illuminates the stair landing with built-in seat. Pegs for hanging coats are set into the horizontal bands. All of the woodwork is stained a deep coffee color. Yes, it's dark. It's supposed to be dark.

ABOVE: A double-gable bungalow with a pop-up graces a side street in Eagle Rock, California. The upturned points on its gables give it a Japanese look. The open porch gable features decorative timberwork supported by groups of timbers resting on stucco piers. The sidewalls are shingled in a ubiquitous southern California pattern. Now painted blue-green, no doubt they were once unpainted. But, unfortunately, once shingles are painted there's no going back, except by re-shingling.

RIGHT: Overlooking the water in Vancouver, British Columbia, this shingled bungalow has an interesting open gable over a pergola on its wraparound porch, supported by slightly tapered, shingled columns. The door and window casings are tapered to match. An oak door with matching sidelights is set off center, and the entry stair comes from the side, possibly because the home is on a corner lot. A pair of windows is set deep inside the gable to let light into the upstairs.

The slightly curved hipped roof of this Milwaukee bungalow is reminiscent of bungalows in India, but the projecting front with its stone-topped Dutch gable comes from somewhere else entirely.

we just wanted to show the very best stuff—it is a coffee table book after all. (Ironic, given that there were no Arts and Crafts coffee tables . . .)

Unlike our other books, this one doesn't have much practical information. Why? Because we want you to buy our other bungalow books—*Bungalow Kitchens, Bungalow Bathrooms, Bungalow Details: Exterior*, and *Bungalow Details: Interior*. All these subjects are complex enough to require their own book. Also, we are

money-grubbing capitalists. I have a bunga-mansion to support, after all.

That is not to say there is no information here at all. Rather, this book deals with the philosophy, history, and influences that led to the bungalow as we know it in North America. Don't worry, it's not very scholarly. Mostly it's a celebration of bungalows and everything on them and in them, and the Arts and Crafts Movement they represent. I think you will enjoy the ride.

The darker brick at the bottom of this two-tone Denver bungalow is capped by a decorative band dividing it from the lighter iron-spotted brick above. Clipped gables on the front and dormers, each supported by five decorative brackets, contrast with the side gable and shed roof over the porch. An original planter sits on the red sandstone that caps the porch piers.

Covered in shingles, a New Jersey bungalow packs a lot of style into a small building. Piers constructed with the same local stone as the chimney flank stone steps with brick risers. On the porch, tapered wood piers anchor a railing of narrow boards alternating with wider pierced boards, and sets of large timbers with fake "tenons" support a side-gabled roof at each corner.

With its brick and limestone trim, tile roof, and art-glass windows, this home is the epitome of a Chicago bungalow. These homes, which number approximately 80,000 in Chicago's "Bungalow Belt," were mostly built in the 1920s. Chicago bungalows sacrificed the large porch of most bungalows in favor of an enlarged sunroom at the front of the living room. The arched basement window, limestone trim, and stylized art glass of the windows are all hallmarks of the style.

ABOVE: Another Denver bungalow shows some English influence in the rolled edges of its fake thatched roof and half-timbered gables. An arched front door with an eyebrow roof adds to the English flavor. Unlike many bungalows, the porch is open, accessed by rounded brick steps. To the right of the porch, a brick planter with trellises brings nature, in the form of climbing roses, close to the dining room windows.

RIGHT: In Memphis, Tennessee, a multi-gabled redbrick bungalow with port cochere shows some fairly elaborate scroll-sawn ornament in the gable peaks, as well as brackets composed of three decoratively sawn boards sandwiched together. A hood of decorative corbels caps three windows bumped out from the facade on the left. Windows and doors with multi-light transoms spread across the rest of the front. One wouldn't think that mint green would go with red brick, but somehow it works.

THE COLOR OF WIND

WHAT IS THE COLOR OF WIND?

ZEN KOAN

Sometimes writing about bungalows is like trying to answer a Zen *koan*. A koan is a paradox or riddle based on the actions or sayings of famous Zen masters. As Alan Watts said, "[It]…is a problem which admits no intellectual solution; the answer has no logical connection with the question, and the question is such a kind as to baffle the intellect altogether." The most famous koan is "What is the sound of one hand clapping?" But I prefer this one:

"The library assistant approached the Zen librarian and said, 'I can't find *Thinking Outside the Box*—it's not on the shelf and not checked out.' The Zen librarian replied, 'If you can't find the box, think outside the chicken.'" (James Quinn)

The idea of a koan is that the Zen student contemplating the puzzle will "think outside the chicken" and, in a moment of sudden understanding, attain *satori*, or enlightenment.

City homes by their very nature tended to be tall and thin, because the lots were small. Though this home is an Arts and Crafts home, and has many features in common with bungalows, it is not a bungalow, being more than one story, and residing on a narrow city lot near downtown Vancouver, British Columbia. Nonetheless, it shares many stylistic features with bungalows, including the exposed rafter tails, gable brackets, and large timbers supporting the porch and the room above it, and the combination of bevel and shingle siding. The saturated paint colors on the exterior are typical of Vancouver. Note how the vanilla-colored trim harmonizes with the deep burgundy of the siding, especially compared to the bright white used along the steps.

The 1911 Lanterman House in La Cañada-Flintridge is a typical California bungalow, at least on the outside. But its multiple gables, projecting bays, surrounding pergolas, and brackets bear little resemblance to the bungalow's Indian antecedents. On the other hand, the surrounding tropical-looking gardens would be right at home in the bungalow's native land of India.

In the same way, I am hoping that by reading and contemplating the photographs in this book, you too will have a moment of bungalow satori, in which it will make perfect sense that a temporary hut from India was transformed in California into an iconic and original house form based on a Socialist design movement originating in nineteenth-century Britain. Or at least you'll be able to recognize a bungalow when you see one.

Architecture isn't simple. Any given house represents the convergence of *plan* or *type* (how the house is arranged—types include four-square, I-house, shotgun, hall-and-parlor, etc.), *time period* (for instance, Victorian is a time period, not a type of house), and decorative *style* (the shape of the box and the stuff that's on it and in it—a house of the Victorian time period might be Italianate, Second Empire, or Queen Anne in style). Complicated enough for most things. But bungalows add a fourth dimension and that is philosophy. Although bungalows have an informal plan, are of a certain time period, and come in different *styles* (Craftsman, California, Japanesque, Swiss Chalet, Prairie, Rustic, and so forth), they are also based on a philosophy that is the foundation for how they were built and furnished, how people expected to live in them, and how the residents related to the larger society.

Bungalows didn't go straight from being a temporary bamboo and thatch hut in Bengal to being a widespread architectural representation of the Arts and Crafts Movement in America. Instead, the original hut was transformed over time and

LEFT: Probably built around the same time as the Lanterman House, a wood-sided bungalow in Vancouver, British Columbia, shares similar stylistic attributes in its gables, brackets, and vine-covered porch. Though much smaller than its southern California cousin, this house is part of the same Arts and Crafts tradition.

BELOW: An old photo shows a 1919 thatch-roofed bungalow in the State of Perak in Western Malaysia, which was also colonized by the British. Raised up on piers, the home's verandah wraps around at least three sides. Notice the slatted vents and lattice work just below the edge of the roofline. The verandah itself is decorated with wicker furniture. To the right, a thatched outbuilding of unknown use abuts the porch. One of the residents poses with her dog on the front lawn. It took the Malaysians rather longer to get rid of the British—till 1957, in fact.

Twin gables like the ones on this Seattle home are typical of bungalows nationwide. Tapered wooden pillars on sturdy piers of local stone are echoed in the tapered uprights of the porch railing. In the gables, wooden knee braces support the wide overhangs of the roof. The sidewall shingle pattern of alternating wide and narrow exposures is also quite common. Multiple lights in the upper window sashes combine with a single light in the lower sashes in a very prevalent type of bungalow window. Yet a bungalow is far more than the sum of these simple parts.

through various filters and interpretations to become the bungalow we know today. It is rather like the game "telephone," where a whispered message is passed along until it ultimately bears little resemblance to the original message. As with bungalows, the end result is often amusing, or at least interesting.

GOING NATIVE

The original Bengali hut, called a *banggolo* or *bangala*, resembled an overturned ship, with a curved roof that extended nearly all the way to the ground. These huts, constructed for temporary use, utilized bamboo and thatch, though more permanent structures were also built with mud walls and constructed on a raised platform (also of dried mud). Roof forms varied, some being pyramid-shaped or hipped, others having gable ends connected by a curving ridge, but all being curved in some way. The walls and floors were smeared with cow dung. As the British colonized India, they adopted (or co-opted) the banggolos. They made some modifications to suit a more European lifestyle, Anglicized the name to "bungalow," and had them built all over India. Eventually they exported the bungalow to other British colonies as a proper sort of housing for Europeans in tropical climates.

Among the modifications made by the British to the original hut was the addition of a verandah (from the Hindu word *varanda*) on four sides of the building. This wraparound porch was often covered by a secondary roof with a slope less steep than that of the main building, though in many cases the main roof covered the verandah as well. Corner areas of the verandah were sometimes walled off for sleeping rooms or bathrooms. The British kept the raised platform, or plinth, which often served as the floor of the verandah. The curved rooflines were abandoned in favor of straight-sided pyramidal or hipped roofs, which were said to have been taken from the standard-issue army tent. Walls were made of brick or mud, often plastered. They added wooden doors and glass-paned windows, where the Indian huts used only hanging mats, and cloth ceilings in the interior to keep vermin from the thatch out of the living areas. The smearing with cow dung was discontinued, being offensive to European sensibilities. Later on, as the Indians began to be rather more aggressive about ending British rule,

> CORNER AREAS OF
> THE VERANDAH WERE
> SOMETIMES WALLED OFF
> FOR SLEEPING ROOMS
> OR BATHROOMS.

Though considerably larger than the first British bungalows, the Pratt House in Ojai, California, designed by architects Charles and Henry Greene, had a similar sort of relaxed resort living in mind, as evidenced by the profusion of porches and terraces that surround it. Having more Japanese than Indian influence, it is nonetheless still within the bungalow milieu.

ABOVE: The walkways of a Pasadena bungalow court are lushly planted with palms, roses, and flowering shrubs, all of which thrive in the warm southern California climate.

RIGHT: The low-pitched roof and deep wraparound front porch of a Memphis bungalow provide a perfect place for relaxing during hot weather. The side gabled roof of this home continues down over the porch, though a glimpse of an off-center hipped dormer is just visible on the left. Limestone pillars and a low wall separate the semiprivate porch space from the public space of the front yard and the street.

the flammable thatched roofs were replaced by tile.

The Anglo-Indian bungalows were primarily built in compounds outside of cities, or in the hill country where the British went to get away from the stifling heat of the low-lands. So, even in India, the bungalow was essentially a suburban or country house.

GETTING AWAY FROM IT ALL

As travel to India became easier in the mid-nineteenth century and communications improved, accounts of life in bungalows began to filter back to England. In a country beginning to feel both the good and bad effects of the Industrial Revolution, the bungalow and the life lived in it seemed exotic and romantic. For the (upper-class) British, the idea of living far from crowding, pollution, class struggle, increasing urbanization, and the complexities of life, and instead having a simple home surrounded by gardens full of exotic tropical plants, and servants that waited on you hand and foot,

seemed like a very fine thing. (The Indians, one is sure, had a different view.) It occurred to a few people in Britain that building a bungalow at home would allow one some of the benefits of the idealized life without actually going to the trouble and expense of traveling to India. To others it presented the possibility of profit, never to be excluded as a motivating factor.

The British, struggling with the conversion from a primarily agrarian economy to an industrial one, had already become nostalgic for an idealized agrarian past. Even some of the lower classes were probably nostalgic for it, having given up their relatively self-directed farming or artisan pursuits to work long hours in factories and live in crowded and unsanitary cities. But for the upper classes, the growing middle class, and, by the end of the century, even some members of the working class, the Industrial Revolution brought increased disposable income as well as more leisure time. This led to the development of specialized resort towns, which in Britain were mainly seaside resorts, and that is where the first British bungalows were built. Interestingly enough, these five bungalows, built in 1869-1870 at Birchington in Kent, resembled American bungalows built from 1900-1930 far more than British bungalows that were built after the turn of the twentieth century. The first bungalows featured low-pitched gable roofs supported by brackets, simple fenestration, a combination of siding materials, and large porches. Their simplicity, though partly an aesthetic choice, had much to do with the increasing difficulty of finding and keeping servants, who had begun to opt for the (relative) freedom of jobs in the factories and mills.

Part of the reason the resort towns were located along the coast had to do with changing ideas about health. Earlier resorts were mainly located at inland towns with mineral hot springs, such as Bath. "Taking the waters" at such places had actually been going on since the Romans, but fashionable ideas about the health benefits of seawater, both immersing

> THE BRITISH, STRUGGLING WITH THE CONVERSION FROM A PRIMARILY AGRARIAN ECONOMY TO AN INDUSTRIAL ONE, HAD ALREADY BECOME NOSTALGIC FOR AN IDEALIZED AGRARIAN PAST.

The romantic feel of an English cottage is evoked by the rolled eaves (imitating thatch), half-timbering, and casement windows of a Denver bungalow. Notice the very subtle notching of the fascia boards on the gable. In a real English cottage, the timbers in the gable would be real structural members, filled in with either brick, stone, or wattle and daub (a form of plaster or stucco).

oneself in it and also drinking it (not recommended), led to new resorts opening up along the English Channel close to London. Patronized by the aristocracy and upper classes, these resorts were only superficially about health—mostly they were about socializing and showing off (as indeed, many resorts of this type still are). Gradually, however, the thinking began to change from the benefits of seawater to the benefits of breathing the sea air. No doubt much of this had to do with concerns about tuberculosis and other contagious diseases, which were believed, in the era before germ theory, to be caused by "miasmas" and "bad air," as well as exposure to large numbers of people in cities or at public assemblies (some truth to that). This belief also led to an emphasis on privacy in leisure, rather than social interaction with large numbers of people, which was emphasized at the earlier resorts—although an influx of less affluent visitors to the older resorts could also have reinforced the idea of privacy. (One must keep oneself above the riff-raff, after all.)

The desire for privacy may also have been driven by a perceived lack of privacy in the cities. New means of communication like the telegraph and the telephone, and transportation like the railroad, allowed people more access to each other. Obviously, this had a good side and a bad side. For the Victorians, it was probably the equivalent of our own love/hate relationship with modern communication devices like cell phones and e-mail, and we can probably relate to their need to "get away from it all."

The leisure home needed to be different from homes in the city to enhance the feeling of getting away from it all. It needed to be less formal, it needed to be out of the ordinary. Even before bungalows, the tendency had been to make country homes picturesque, and the nostalgia for the countryside cottages of pre-industrial Britain was widespread among the upper classes. The bungalow was like a cottage, and yet it was exotic and foreign as well. It fit the bill perfectly.

In the space of about ten years, bungalows had spread from the seaside resorts to other

Along the New Jersey shore, a seaside bungalow features unusual round projections on either end of the porch, each topped by a gable roof rather than the conical roof one might expect, and supported by slender columns of local stone atop walls of the same. The rest of the home is quite austere, with only a small decorative cutout at the ends of the fascia boards, and little other ornamentation.

areas of the country, where they were built as weekend getaways for upper middle class city dwellers. This is a practice that has continued right up to our own time, when people who can afford it have second homes in resort areas for weekend and summer vacations.

THE SEEDS OF CHANGE

But the desire to live simply and get away from the cities on occasion was not the only reaction to industrialization. Changing ideas about nature were also happening. In an agrarian society, nature is usually respected and feared. In the increasingly industrial society, people no longer lived in a natural environment, so they began to idealize Nature, which was now capitalized—either way, it was from the distance, perhaps even from the safety of the porch. Competing, and often diametrically opposed, ideas about society, the arts, politics, economics, health, morality, and other issues were also fueled by the changing times. Concepts such as Adam Smith's laissez-faire capitalism, Darwin's origin of species, Louis Pasteur's germ theory were all either promulgated or widely adopted in the nineteenth century. Surprisingly, in the late 1700s, philosopher and economist Adam Smith realized that assembly lines were efficient, but would likely lead to an unhappy workforce, as individuals were forced to do mundane and repetitive tasks all day. He thought that offering education to workers would blunt their dissatisfaction. No one, of course, thought to ask the workers.

Others had different ideas about the way to deal with the rise of industrialization. The architect Augustus Welby Northmore Pugin was the first to decry industrialism and call for a return to the architecture and hand craftsmanship of the Middle Ages. He believed that art and architecture had the capacity to improve society. At about the same time, the Pre-Raphaelite Brotherhood was rebelling against the kind of painting favored by the Royal Academy, which was described

A somewhat larger bungalow in Denver is also based on English cottage architecture, this time with a faux thatch roof composed of bent and eccentrically laid wood shingles. Clipped gables on all the dormers (sometimes called a jerkinhead or shreadhead roof) add to the cottage feel.

as "Cattle-pieces and sea-pieces and fruit-pieces and family-pieces, the eternal brown cows in ditches, and white sails in squalls, and sliced lemons in saucers, and foolish faces in simpers." They supported instead paintings that harkened back to the time before the Renaissance, in other words, pre-Raphael. The official Brotherhood, consisting of William Holman Hunt, Dante Gabriel Rossetti, John Everett Millais, and some less famous guys with three names, also had an unofficial circle of like-minded artists, architects, poets, and other creative types, which included Ford Madox Brown, Edward Coley Burne-Jones, Phillip Webb, and William Morris.

Defending the Pre-Raphaelites and building on the ideals of Pugin was John Ruskin, an artist, poet, philosopher, scientist, environmentalist, art critic, and professor, who was to influence a whole generation of nineteenth-century artists and designers. Ruskin's ideals were summed up thus, in an 1872 issue of *Vanity Fair*:

"He sees in the universal desire to make money exclude every other object of exertion the great and fatal evil of the times, and rebels entirely against all the complex social and political arrangements which have been constituted into a system to that end. He holds that to rely on manufactures for greatness is to lean upon a broken reed, and that England must live upon herself through agriculture if ever she would return to a healthy condition of existence. So convinced is he of this that he has given a tenth part of his fortune to

The living room at Artemisia features an even larger oak-paneled fireplace, also with Batchelder tile, and just to the left of it, behind a set of elaborately scroll-sawn doors, lie some of the pipes for the home's pipe organ. Not exactly a proponent of the simple life, the home's builder owned a construction company, so he was showing off a little. Okay, a lot.

found a colony in which Englishmen shall be developed, through the alternation of agricultural labour with artistic pursuits, into the better specimens of humanity which he believes can thus alone be produced. That he will ever see his opinions adopted or even seriously entertained is not to be expected; but by those who have not bowed the knee to the modern Baal he will be gratefully remembered as one preaching in the wilderness the abandonment of the grosser things of life and the realisation of the Ideal."

It is ironic that Ruskin, the great proponent of medievalism, was what we would term a Renaissance man.

In the 1850s, Morris and Burne-Jones, under the influence of Rossetti, gave up their Oxford theology studies to focus on painting, and moved to a studio in Red Lion Square, London. The need to furnish the studio soon had Morris designing some medieval-style furniture, which was decorated with paintings by various members of the group. They discovered they liked working together, and it was all downhill from there. They began to refine their ideas while they worked on Red House, the house Morris was having built for himself and his new bride, Jane Burden. Almost as a joke, they decided to form a commercial company of "Fine Art Workmen", to be known as Morris, Marshall, Faulkner and Company, that worked in stained glass, mural decoration, carving, metalwork, furniture, and embroidery. Through the work of "The Firm", as they called it, the seeds of ideas about art, design, and social and political reform, planted by Pugin and Ruskin, began to sprout and eventually flower in what became known as the Arts and Crafts Movement.

ABOVE: The middle panel of a tripartite art-glass window on a shingled Arts and Crafts home in Vancouver, B.C., displays a turreted castle surrounded by trees, while the side panels have abstracted roses reminiscent of the designs of the Scottish Arts and Crafts architect Charles Rennie MacIntosh. This kind of window, with a large fixed center sash flanked by two smaller operable windows, originated on turn-of-the-twentieth-century Chicago commercial buildings and is often called a Chicago window.

RIGHT: Though much simpler than the stained glass designed by Morris and Company, stained glass became a staple of Arts and Crafts decoration, showing up in the windows, doors, built-ins, and light fixtures of bungalows large and small. An oak door with sidelights on a Victoria, British Columbia, bungalow features art glass in a stylized tulip pattern. The door hardware, mailbox, and light fixture are new, crafted by the homeowners' company, Waterglass Studios.

IN FULL FLOWER

John Ruskin may have been a Renaissance man, but he had nothing on William Morris. Maybe it was because they were the only two men of the nineteenth century who didn't have three or four names. Morris was an artist, designer, poet, writer, craftsman, typographer, illustrator, painter, book printer, weaver, embroiderer, dyer, craftsman, interior designer, businessman, merchant, historic preservationist, garden designer, environmentalist, and staunch Socialist. And not necessarily in that order. He mastered the design and production of stained glass, wallpaper, carpets, tapestry, printed and woven textiles, wallpaper, embroidery, furniture, books, ceramic tiles, calligraphy, murals, woodcuts, and even linoleum. His lifelong friend Edward Burne-Jones summed up Morris's career in these words:

> "When I first knew Morris nothing would content him but being a monk, and getting to Rome, and then he must be an architect, and apprenticed himself to Street, and worked for two years, but when I came up to London and began to paint he threw it all up, and must paint too, and then he must give it up and make poems, and then he must give it up and make window hangings and pretty things, and when he had achieved that, he must be a poet again, and then after two or three years of Earthly Paradise time, he

The Morris wallpaper pattern *Chrysanthemum* accents the wall behind the headboard in an attic bedroom of a Seattle bungalow, and simple curtains of matching fabric hang at the windows. The reddish tone of the Douglas fir trim and beams harmonizes with the similar color of the English Arts and Crafts bed, which features dark-stained insets carved with highly stylized flowers.

LEFT: In the dining room of the same bungalow, another Morris pattern called *Compton* (actually designed by Morris's assistant and successor, John Henry Dearle) covers the walls between the plate rail and the box beam ceiling. The paper helps harmonize the color of the Douglas fir woodwork and the various wood tones of the furniture. Seen through the colonnade, the living room is simple, using only a green stenciled design in the corners of the otherwise plain walls. Although Morris's designs seem naturalistic compared to the even more abstracted florals favored by the American Arts and Crafts Movement, they were still quite simple in comparison to their florid Victorian counterparts.

BELOW: The walls of a bedroom in a Berkeley Arts and Crafts home are covered with contemporary paper designed by artist Carol Mead, based on an 1891 paper by Lewis F. Day, a contemporary of William Morris and one of the founders of the Art Workers Guild, along with Walter Crane and W. R. Lethaby. The furniture pieces are reproductions by Davis and Moss of furniture found in the attic of Morris's home at Kelmscott Manor. The furniture was designed by Ford Madox Brown and produced by Morris and Company. The original furniture did not include a chair, so Audel Davis designed a chair to go with the other pieces. The reproductions did not gain wide acceptance in the Arts and Crafts Revival, obsessed as it is with fumed oak and matte green pottery, so no doubt these pieces will be valuable and rare in a hundred years.

must learn dyeing, and lived in a vat, and learned weaving, and knew all about looms, and then made more books, and learned tapestry, and then wanted to smash everything up and begin the world anew, and now it is printing he cares for, and to make wonderful rich-looking books, and all things he does splendidly—and if he lives the printing will have an end— but not I hope, before Chaucer and the Morte d'Arthur are done, and then he'll do I don't know what, but every minute will be alive."

Reverence for beauty and nature, and a belief that beautiful houses and buildings could have a profound effect on the people in them was central to Morris's worldview. Each of the things he took up, he took up with passion and intensity, yet each thread, be it stained glass or Socialism, was part of a larger tapestry, an attempt to have a truly integrated life, and to offer an example to others that an integrated life was possible, even amidst the social and class struggle of his own society. He wanted to reform the decorative arts, to return to them the respect he felt they had enjoyed in an earlier time, before the arts had been separated into Fine Arts (painting and sculpture) and Decorative Arts (everything else). As a Socialist, he wanted to change society and politics. These two aspirations were not contradictory in his view.

This was a formidable undertaking, to say the least. The Victorian middle classes, having access for the first time to the sort of sumptuous furniture and objects that previously only

LEFT: This elaborately carved sideboard is the sort of furniture that probably would have reduced Morris to a fit of violent retching—useless ornament taken to extremes. Let's see, it has birds, gryphons, cherubs, lions, muscular guys with beards, faces, flowers, drapery, and miscellaneous carving. Oh, and a mirror. With all that as a background, it's hard to notice the rather beautiful collection of Tiffany-style art glass vases on top.

Though the objects in this Seattle parlor are individually lovely, and probably of a higher quality than much that was produced during the Victorian period, the shear volume of objects is visually overwhelming, not to mention that there is basically nowhere to sit, since all the chairs and settees are covered with pillows and scarves and paintings. This kind of décor induced the same sort of horror in the Arts and Crafts devotees that a shag-carpeted room full of Day-Glo velvet Elvis paintings might provoke for people of taste in this century.

ABOVE: A reproduction Kelmscott Manor settle sits in front of a concrete brick fireplace in this Berkeley home, while an oak bookcase to the right holds art pottery as well as books. Next to the window, a plein-air painting hangs over a Kelmscott reproduction table and chair. On the mantel, art pottery and candlesticks share the space with an Arts and Crafts clock. Morris would have approved of the austerity of this room, as well as the Oriental rugs on the floor, as he was quite an authority on Oriental rugs and helped advise the South Kensington Museum (now the Victoria and Albert Museum) on the purchase of rugs for their collection.

OPPOSITE: Somewhat less overwrought than the Seattle parlor on page 45, this modest Victorian in Portland, Oregon, nonetheless wins the award for most amusing portieres (door curtains). At least there is somewhere to sit, and of course the parlor has a piano, necessary for entertainment in the pre-radio and television era.

the rich could afford, didn't really care that it was machine-made, often of poor quality, and in extremely dubious taste. They bought lots of it, and manufacturers were happy to supply it. So the mission of Morris and the other reformers was complex: to educate the public and reshape popular taste, to reform the means of production and consumption, and by this, to change the structure of society. Piece of cake.

Morris and his cohorts may have idealized the past, though they were hardly alone in this. In a lecture in 1888, Morris described the craftsman of the Middle Ages:

"Here, then, is a strange contrast, which I most seriously invite you to consider, between the craftsman of the Middle Ages and him of to-day. The medieval man sets to work at his own time, in his own house; probably makes his tool, instrument, or simple machine himself, even before he gets on to his web, or his lump of clay, or what not. What ornament there shall

ABOVE: A Kelmscott settle is flooded with light streaming through three large arched windows in a Berkeley home. Flanked by two oak Arts and Crafts bookcases (a glimpse of the mandatory thru-tenons can be seen near the top of the right-hand bookcase), the settle is softened by embroidered and printed pillows, while an oak floor lamp with a stained-glass shade (by craftsman Michael Adams) stands ready to provide light in the evenings.

RIGHT: A reproduction Kelmscott Manor bed is an island of serenity in the attic bedroom of a Berkeley bungalow. A simple white matelassé coverlet is covered with a crazy-quilt throw, and the leaded-glass window looks out over the trees. The hand-hammered copper lamp on the bedside table is from Dirk Van Erp's Copper Shop, though it was actually made by his wife, Agatha.

ABOVE: A high-back settle (thought to be of Scandinavian origin) with a cut-out apron below the cushion complements the Kelmscott settle in front of the leaded-glass windows of a Berkeley bungalow. On either side, cabinets built by the homeowner hold stereo equipment and provide display space for a collection of Indian pottery on top. A Navajo rug anchors the space.

LEFT: A reproduction Kelmscott table is tucked into a corner under a painting by artist Ray Strong. The matching chair (there was no chair with the original Kelmscott furniture) was designed by present-day craftsman Audel Davis.

be on his finished work he himself determines, and his mind and hand designs it and carries it out; tradition, that is to say the minds and thoughts of all workmen gone before, this, in its concrete form of the custom of his craft, does indeed guide and help him; otherwise he is free."

Morris has often been called the founder of the Arts and Crafts Movement, though obviously he didn't do it single-handedly. (The name, Arts and Crafts, actually originated with an exhibition staged in London by the Arts and Crafts Exhibition Society in 1888.) Nonetheless, his contributions and the inspiration they provided (and continue to provide) cannot be overlooked. A few years after his death in 1896, Lewis F. Day wrote, "He it was that snatched from the hand of Ruskin the torch which Pugin earlier in the century had kindled and fired the love of beauty in us."

Morris was a brilliant designer; his textiles and wallpaper have been in continuous production since he designed them. Many of the typefaces he created are also still in use. He is largely responsible for reviving many craft processes, such as vegetable dyeing, tapestry weaving, and manuscript illumination, which were on the verge of being lost. Interestingly enough, the adjustable-back chair, which now bears his name, was actually designed by Phillip Webb, based on a sketch of a chair an associate had seen in the workshop of Ephraim Colman, a carpenter in Sussex. The design was popular and was widely copied.

It is difficult to comprehend from our viewpoint in the twenty-first century just how radical William Morris was. As Americans, it is difficult to comprehend the rigid divisions of the British class system, especially in the nineteenth century, living as we do in a country where class distinctions are far more sub-tle and somewhat more fluid. Even as Morris called for an end to class divisions, he retained many of the prejudices of his upper middle-class upbringing. Yet, he did his best to treat his workers well and pay them fairly, and was apparently what we would call a "hands-on, roll up your sleeves" sort of manager. Certainly he shared the

Who needs a recliner when you can have a much more tasteful leather-upholstered Morris chair with a matching ottoman, as seen here in the living room of a Milwaukee Arts and Crafts home? At the far end of the room, built-in bookcases with leaded-glass doors frame a window seat that also disguises the radiator. A pair of sconces frame a painting by the owner's mother over a green tiled fireplace. The oak woodwork is set off by a stenciled frieze by craftsperson Amy Miller.

Chrysanthemum wallpaper, designed by Morris in 1876, complements the deeply tufted velvet upholstery of the chairs and chaise longue in the study of a Portland, Oregon, Victorian home. By Victorian standards, the décor of this room is relatively spare, although Morris might have looked askance at the shirred, fringed, and tasseled velvet pillow on the chaise.

The English influence in Victoria, British Columbia, is strong, so many of its bungalows manifest that inspiration with clipped gables, half-timbering, diamond-pane windows, and other elements of English cottage design. Though this red-roofed bungalow is tiny, it has a view of the water that its English counterparts might envy, and in spite of that, it might well have been affordable to a working class family when it was first built.

A Berkeley home by architect Bernard Maybeck flaunts its rustic detailing while at the same time the arch-top windows in the gable end and over the doors on the right (barely seen), hint at a more sophisticated kind of architecture that Maybeck was also capable of, having trained at the Academie des Beaux Arts in Paris. Most of Maybeck's homes were built for the upper middle class—university professors, business people, and other professionals. Nonetheless, the ideals filtered down to working-class houses as well.

somewhat condescending attitude toward the poor that most of his contemporaries held, the idea that they would be "uplifted" from their degraded state by art, education, and proper work. Nonetheless, he once said in a lecture, "I do not want art for a few, any more than education for a few, or freedom for a few."

Nor can we really have any idea how radical his design ideas and simple interiors were during his time. In retrospect, most of them look quite overblown and Victorian compared to the sparseness and lack of color that is a hallmark of the majority of current interiors, which we have learned to think of as normal, with their off-white drywall and beige carpeting.

It is also difficult to grasp the extent of his influence, both among his contemporaries and those that followed him. The list of those he influenced or inspired in the fields of art and design is long, the most well-known include William de Morgan,

Walter Crane, Arthur Heygate Mackmurdo, Charles Robert Ashbee, Charles Rennie MacIntosh, Charles Francis Annesley Voysey, and Mackay Hugh Baillie-Scott.

It is the great paradox of the British Arts and Crafts Movement that its emphasis on handwork, quality, and fair pay (the attempts to pay something that resembles a living wage), made its products unaffordable to any but the well-to-do. As a Socialist, Morris could not have been unaware of this. There was some attempt by Morris and Company to provide less expensive products, such as machine-made Axminster rugs, and embroidery designs available as kits, but most of its goods and services remained luxuries for the rich.

A Zen parable states that before enlightenment one must chop wood and carry water, and that after enlightenment one must chop wood and carry water. Although Morris was not a Zen Buddhist, he surely understood the principle:

> "When all is gained that you (and we) so long for, what shall we do then? That great change which we are working for, each in his own way, will come like other changes, as a thief in the night, and will be with us before we know it; but let us imagine that its consummation has come suddenly and dramatically, acknowledged and hailed by all right—minded people; and what shall we do then, lest we begin once more to heap up fresh corruption for the woeful labour of ages once again? I say, as we turn away from the flagstaff where the new banner has been just run up; as we depart, our ears yet ringing with the blare of the heralds' trumpets that have proclaimed the new order of things, what shall we turn to then, what MUST we turn to then?
>
> To what else, save to our work, our daily labour?"

In his own work, Morris clearly experienced what we would now call flow, being so engrossed in the work at hand that consciousness of the outside world or the passage of time disappears. It is a state that cannot be experienced continuously, and to this day there are few people who experience it at work. Morris was certainly realistic enough to understand that as well. Yet he sought for balance and integration in life as well as labor:

LEFT: A festival of purlins, brackets, and railings, as well as an arched hood over the upper-story windows and a second-floor porch, decorate the front of a Milwaukee Arts and Crafts home built of wire-cut brick.

BELOW: Bungalows may well have been the most popular product to come out of the Arts and Crafts Movement, and probably the most successful. Blocks upon blocks in Chicago are lined with rows of Chicago bungalows, a species of bungalow all unto themselves, which were remarkably popular at the time they were built and continue to be admired today. When built, they were affordable to both the middle and working classes, and new immigrants saved up till they were able to move from crowded tenements in the inner city into bungalows in new developments in the suburbs, which are, of course, no longer suburbs but part of the larger city.

"I cannot suppose there is anybody here who would think it either a good life, or an amusing one, to sit with one's hands before one doing nothing—to live like a gentleman, as fools call it.

Nevertheless there IS dull work to be done, and a weary business it is setting men about such work, and seeing them through it, and I would rather do the work twice over with my own hands than have such a job: but now only let the arts which we are talking of beautify our labour, and be widely spread, intelligent, well understood both by the maker and the user, let them grow in one word POPULAR, and there will be pretty much an end of dull work and its wearing slavery; and no man will any longer have an excuse for talking about the curse of labour, no man will any longer have an excuse for evading the blessing of labour. I believe there is nothing that will aid the world's progress so much as the attainment of this; I protest there is nothing in the world that I desire so much as this, wrapped up, as I am sure it is, with changes political and social, that in one way or another we all desire."

Morris got his wish, though not quite in the way he might have wanted. Objects of the Arts and Crafts Movement did become popular, even fashionable, as members of the upper classes began to embrace all things "artistic", from Gothic, Japonisme, and Art Nouveau, to Arts and Crafts, with little regard for underlying philosophy, as often happens when things become popular. Much of this was spurred by new stores offering goods imported from, or inspired by Japan, which had recently been opened to the West. The greatest of these was Arthur Lazenby Liberty's store on London's Regent Street, opened in 1875 (and still in business). Liberty sold silk and porcelain from the Orient, and furniture inspired by the Orient. These proved so popular that Liberty branched out into carpets, clothing, metalware, carpets, and pottery. Unlike the Arts and Crafts designers (though he employed many of them, often without attribution), he was willing to use machinery and mechanized techniques to produce goods in large quantities. Nonetheless, his intention was to refine the public's taste and improve aesthetic standards in Britain.

Above: Bungalows were popular all across North America. The two British Columbian bungalows seen here, obviously built by the same builder (note the similarities), were nonetheless different enough for the owners to feel that their home was unique. The red one has only two pillars, while the yellow one has three. The gable decoration is unique on each one, and the red one has an open porch in its dormer while the yellow one's porch is enclosed with glass. The windows on the side bump-outs also differ.

Left: Much Japanese influence is evident on this unusual Arts and Crafts home in Denver. The broad, flat planes of stucco framed by dark timbers, and the timber framing of the porch gable (which, unlike many bungalows, is actually structural) reflect Japanese building traditions. Yet the sturdy, tapered, brick pillars capped with local sandstone would not be found in Japan. The best features of this house are the unusual dormers cut into the edge of the roofline. One could almost call it a bungalow with a really big pop-top.

ART FOR ART'S SAKE

The popularity of "artistic" objects was also spurred by the Aesthetic Movement (some would say more of a cult), which paralleled the rise of the Arts and Crafts Movement and had some of the same roots—the pre-Raphaelites and the medievalists. It is often confused with the Arts and Crafts Movement, as some of the participants and some of the rhetoric were the same. Rossetti, Oscar Wilde, James Abbott McNeill, Algernon Charles Swinburne, and Aubrey Beardsley were among the well-known proponents. In part, the Aesthetic Movement grew out of ideas put forth by Theophile Gautier and Walter Pater, summed up as "art for art's sake" and the idea that the pursuit of beauty is enough in and of itself. Gautier wrote, "Imagination is the one weapon in the war against reality." Kind of reminds me of the bumper sticker, "Reality is for people who can't handle drugs."

IN MANY RESPECTS THE AESTHETIC MOVEMENT USED THE DESIGNS AND FORMS OF ARTS AND CRAFTS WITHOUT THE UNDERLYING SOCIAL AND POLITICAL PHILOSOPHY.

In many respects the Aesthetic Movement used the designs and forms of Arts and Crafts without the underlying social and political philosophy. It was the triumph of form over substance. The Aesthetes also veered from the Arts and Crafts idea that art could be taught, and that everyone could be creative if given the chance, taking the rather more exclusive view that anything worth knowing, especially art, couldn't be taught, and if the great unwashed masses didn't appreciate its subtleties, well, the hell with them. Given that this was easier than uplifting the masses, and absolved the upper classes of guilt, allowing them to essentially turn their backs on the pressing social problems of the day, it naturally became quite popular.

The "Turkish corner" was popular with the Aesthetes and they happily piled Japanese, Morrocan, Chinese, Egyptian, Indian, Turkish, Middle Eastern, Eastern European, and any other vaguely exotic objects they could find into a corner or nook. It was all very daring and counter-culture for the time. If the 1960s hippies of San Francisco's Haight-Ashbury district had had more money, this is how they would have decorated, though with a few Day-Glo Family Dog posters thrown in for good measure. This Turkish room, in a Seattle home, has some quite lovely objects in it, if you can pick them out of the clutter, and, of course, the requisite hookah. The Aesthetes were nothing if not decadent.

The Aesthetes particularly embraced the decorative arts as the ideal blank canvas on which to project their notions of beauty and refinement. Oscar Wilde wrote, "Mere colour, unspoiled by meaning, and unallied with definite form, can speak to the soul in a thousand different ways…" Aesthetes, with their delicate and cultivated sensibilities, would swoon with ecstasy over a teapot or a sunflower. They used phrases like "utterly utter" and "consummately too too." Naturally

Several wallpapers from Bradbury and Bradbury's Herter Brothers collection decorate the double parlor of a Victorian home in Alameda, California. The Herter Brothers were the premier Victorian decorators in New York during the late-nineteenth century, catering to wealthy clients. Furniture with elaborate marquetry (wood inlay) was their specialty, but they provided everything needed to decorate a room, as the Aesthetes believed that each room should be a unified artistic statement. Panels of stylized sunflowers form the dado (lower third of the wall), while a sunflower frieze tops the wall just below the crown molding. A suite of ebonized furniture upholstered in burgundy velvet completes the picture. Of course, the room isn't really gloomy enough to be properly Aesthetic.

they were ripe for parody. A cartoon in Punch showed an aesthetic bride and groom inspecting a teapot. "It is quite consummate, is it not?" asks the groom. "It is indeed!" replies the bride. "Oh, Algernon, let us live up to it!" Gilbert and Sullivan also lampooned the Aesthetes in their operetta, Patience, where one character exclaims, "There is a transcendentality of delirium—an acute accentuation of supremest ecstasy—which the Earthy might easily mistake for indigestion. But it is not indigestion—it is aesthetic transfiguration!"

Though lacking the underlying philosophy of Arts and Crafts, many of the products of the Aesthetic Movement were nonetheless very beautiful, and it may not be entirely wrong to love beauty for its own sake. In an 1882 lecture tour in America, Wilde defended the Aesthetic Movement:

> "If you ask nine-tenths of the British public what is the meaning of the word aesthetics, they will tell you it is the French for affectation or the German for a dado... to disagree with three-fourths of the British public on all points is one of the first elements of sanity, one of the deepest consolations in all moments of spiritual doubt.
>
> You have heard, I think, a few of you, of two flowers connected with the Aesthetic Movement in England, and said (I assure you, erroneously) to be the food of some aesthetic young men. Well, let me tell you that the reason we love the lily and the sunflower, in spite of what Mr. Gilbert may tell you, is not for any vegetable fashion at all. It is because these two lovely flowers are in England the two most perfect models of design, the most naturally adapted for decorative art—the gaudy leonine beauty of the one and the precious loveliness of the other giving to the artist the most entire and perfect joy. And so with you: let there be no flower in your meadows that does not wreathe its tendrils around your pillows, no little leaf in your Titan forests that does not lend its form to design, no curving spray of wild rose or brier that does not live for ever in carven arch or window or marble, no bird in your air that is not giving the

The same Bradbury paper in a blue color graces a bedroom in a San Francisco Victorian home. A blue-and-white vase (blue-and-white pottery was also big with the Aesthetes) in the corner holds actual sunflowers, and peacock feathers are well represented on the bedcovering. A few pieces of ebonized Anglo Japanesque furniture and the all-important palm plant (a feature of any Victorian interior) fill out the room.

ABOVE: A brick bungalow with rolled eaves imitating thatch (here rendered in bentwood shingles) certainly has an English cottage look that might fit right in at the seaside in Britain, though it is actually located in Denver. Arch-top casement windows are echoed by the front door and tiny eyebrow dormer on the roof.

A certain English influence is also detectable on this Milwaukee bungalow, especially its leaded-glass windows and the flattened arches. There is even a rather medieval-torch look to the iron light fixtures flanking the front door.

The dark brickwork, which is quite elaborate on the chimney, lend a certain medieval aspect to a Denver bungalow. Intricate brickwork is a hallmark of many Denver bungalows, built mostly by Italian masons.

iridescent wonder of its colour, the exquisite curves of its wings in flight, to make more precious the preciousness of simple adornment. For the voices that have their dwelling in sea and mountain are not the chosen music of liberty only. Other messages are there in the wonder of wind-swept heights and the majesty of silent deep—messages that, if you will listen to them, will give you the wonder of all new imagination, the treasure of all new beauty."

Mr. Wilde was a pretty good writer.

THE BOHEMIAN LIFE

The bungalows being built at the seaside had begun to acquire a "bohemian" reputation, especially after a hotel was built at Westgate in 1879 and decorated in what was then avant-garde London taste—wallpapers by Christopher Dresser and Walter Crane. Rossetti died in a Birchington bungalow in 1882. By then, bungalows had come to represent the ideal of "the simplification of life" and "getting back to nature." But most of the houses by British Arts and Crafts architects were not bungalows. They may have been one story, but they looked to British vernacular houses and medieval prototypes as inspiration. It was not until the bungalow was exported to North America that it became the architectural symbol of the American Arts and Crafts Movement.

SMILING LAWNS AND TASTEFUL COTTAGES

The Gothic Revival had made its way across the Atlantic by the mid-nineteenth century and was popularized through the pattern books of A.J. Downing, A.J. Davis, and others. Downing wrote in the preface to one of his books, "There are three excellent reasons why my countrymen should have good houses. The first, is because a good house (and by this I mean a fitting, tasteful, and significant dwelling) is a powerful means of civilization. A nation, whose rural population is content to live in mean huts and miserable hovels, is certain to be behind its neighbors in education, the arts, and all that makes up the external signs of progress. With the perception of proportion, symmetry, order and beauty, awakens the desire for possession, and with them comes that refinement of manners which distinguishes a civilized from a coarse and brutal people. But, when smiling lawns and tasteful cottages begin to embellish a country, we know that order and culture are established. And as the first incentive towards this change is awakened in the minds of most men by the perception of beauty and superiority in external objects, it must follow that the interest manifested in the Rural Architecture of a country like this, has much to do with the progress of its civilization."

Pierced gable ornaments like the one on the side of this Vancouver, B.C., bungalow were another device picked up from the Gothic Revival. This particular home has an interesting combination gable/shed dormer, as well as an arch set between its three-timber pillars. And let me reiterate: just because other people choose to paint their trim white does not mean it's the right thing to do.

ABOVE: The wide bargeboards (fascia boards) on the gable ends of Gothic Revival houses show up again on bungalows, although the influence of Switzerland, Germany, and the Scandinavian countries, which also have a tradition of decorative bargeboards, cannot be discounted. The two-inch-thick fascia boards on this Denver bungalow have been sawn and notched and scalloped within an inch of their lives, as have the exposed rafter tails. The brackets are fairly complicated as well, and "held together" with fake "pegs" at sides and bottom.

RIGHT: More scallops and notching decorate the fascia board on the garage of the same bungalow (above), and cutouts embellish the gable vent. It is unclear whether the silhouette (a cat?) cut into the vent was part of the original design or a later addition.

Gothic Revival in America tended to be rendered in wood rather than stone (sometimes known as Carpenter Gothic), but the exposed decorative structural elements, wide bargeboards, and brackets, would eventually find their way, in a modified form, onto the later bungalows. The fashion for exposed structure also led to the Stick style, from which bungalows borrowed elements as well.

British goods by Morris and others were already being sold in America in the mid-nineteenth century, mostly without the accompanying philosophy. But the influences that led to the American Arts and Crafts Movement really began to coalesce around the time of the Centennial Exhibition, held in Philadelphia in 1876. The exhibition resulted in a surge of American pride, as well as the realization that up to that point there had not been art or architecture that really reflected American culture and aspirations.

> **THE FASHION FOR EXPOSED STRUCTURE ALSO LED TO THE STICK STYLE, FROM WHICH BUNGALOWS BORROWED ELEMENTS AS WELL.**

ABOVE: Decorative structural elements that started with the Gothic Revival became a defining characteristic of later bungalows. Here, a bungalow in Vancouver, British Columbia, designed by Jud Yoho, a Seattle builder and publisher of the *Bungalow Magazine* from 1911–16, makes use of notched four-by-four-inch timbers stacked like Lincoln Logs™ to form piers for this shingled bungalow.

LEFT: A plethora of exposed corbels, rafter tails, and brackets trim a Milwaukee Arts and Crafts home. But the most noticeable details are the carved lion heads on the brackets, crafted by one of Milwaukee's German woodcarvers.

We had been content to copy or import styles from Europe. A tableau of a pre-Revolutionary War kitchen at the exhibition kindled an interest in America's colonial past.

The pavilions of various foreign countries, particularly Britain, Sweden, Switzerland, and Japan, as well as the products shown, influenced artists and architects including Henry Hobson Richardson and Stanford White. The British pavilion, a half-timbered building in British vernacular style, the Swiss building in the form of a chalet, the Swedish pavilion constructed of logs, and the tiled roof and upturned eaves of the Japanese pavilion were all to influence American architecture in the late-nineteenth and early-twentieth centuries. The exhibition was a great success, though later critics didn't think kindly of it:

Critics today look back upon the Centennial Exhibition as an architectural and artistic calamity that produced not a single new idea but was, rather, the epitome of accumulated bad taste of the era that was called the Gilded Age, the Tragic Era, the Dreadful Decade, or the Pragmatic Acquiescence, depending on which epithet you thought most searing.

Russell Lyons, *The Tastemakers*, 1954

ABOVE: With apologies to Jerry Lee Lewis, the exterior of Artemisia, a large Arts and Crafts mansion in Hollywood, has "a whole lotta structure goin' on." That's a lot of four by fours just to hold up a window box. The brackets above the window support a beam that technically holds up the roof overhang, although that much structure is hardly required. This is the kind of thing that makes me love bungalows so much.

RIGHT: Another Vancouver bungalow shows very typical knee braces, half-timbering with roughcast stucco infill, and simple tapered porch columns. Do I have to repeat myself about the white trim?

The structure on this bungalow in Milwaukee is all fake, but apparently it still took six "pegs" to wedge all those "thru-tenons" in the fascia board. And I can't repeat this enough: Do not use the color white on the outside of a house. Ever.

The Queen Anne style, which had nothing to do with Queen Anne, was also borrowed from Britain. In Britain, it was more of a Jacobean Revival, favored by architects like Richard Norman Shaw, considered to be the originator of the style. In America, the style, which was also called "Old English," came to be characterized by bewildering excess, featuring large projecting bay windows, towers, turrets, porches (often on multiple stories), balconies, stained glass decorations, roof finials and crestings, wall carvings and/or inset panels of stone or terra-cotta, cantilevered upper stories, acres of decorative trim, patterned shingles, belt courses, elaborate brackets, banisters and spindles…. It's the sort of house most people think of as the typical house of the Victorian period.

All of these influences combined to result in the houses now known as Shingle style, though that name was not applied to them until the 1950s. As one would expect, they are clad in shingles. Shingle style houses feature asymmetrical roof forms and massing, often with towers and projecting bays, but in a much-simplified form compared to Queen Anne houses. The interiors were more open and spacious than in other

Vednesday Afternoon Club House, Alhambra, Cal.

ABOVE: This is another of my favorite buildings, the Wednesday Afternoon Club House in Alhambra, California (near Pasadena). Also influenced by Swiss architecture, this building has the biggest honking brackets I've ever seen, as well as a really fine pair of Arts and Crafts–style double doors. But look closely at the ground just to the right of the tree—there is a miniature model of the building right next to the porch. I don't know why it's there, but it's really fabulous. Unfortunately, this amazing building was torn down in the 1960s.

RIGHT: Actually, for a Queen Anne–style house, this home in Alameda, California, is pretty tame, having only one tower and a couple of rounded porches. Though how could one fail to be amused by the gigantic scrolled corbels at the bottom of the entry stairs?

ABOVE: Both Japanese and Swiss influences are combined on a Berkeley Arts and Crafts home, though it looks like the architect may also have been influenced by Pasadena architects Charles and Henry Greene. A closer look at the front facade reveals its asymmetry, which is not immediately apparent. Unfortunately, since this home was built, one of the subsequent owners opted to paint the inside bright white.

RIGHT: Just for comparison, here is the Thorsen House, the only house in Berkeley designed by Greene and Greene. It shares the same Japanese influence as the previous home, though obviously rendered larger and more expensively. The hillside lot has a commanding view of the Golden Gate and the San Francisco Bay, so the Greenes chose to use large picture windows to take in the view, though still with their signature "cloud lift" muntins, taken from Japanese design. The home is L-shaped on its corner lot, providing a sheltered garden in back, important for late summer afternoons in Berkeley, where the fog often creeps in with accompanying wind. Some homes by the Greene brothers are often referred to as "ultimate bungalows," though they are not really bungalows at all, for all that they may be ultimate. The Greenes were masterful architects, and their homes were some of the finest produced during the Arts and Crafts era.

A clear Swiss influence is at work on the scalloped eaves and twin gable dormer of a Berkeley bungalow.
The only thing missing is the window boxes full of red geraniums.

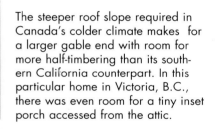

The steeper roof slope required in Canada's colder climate makes for a larger gable end with room for more half-timbering than its southern California counterpart. In this particular home in Victoria, B.C., there was even room for a tiny inset porch accessed from the attic.

The cut-out designs of the balcony railing on the second floor of a chalet-style Denver home would be right at home in Switzerland, though probably with less emphasis on thru-tenons. One can only be astounded at the size and complexity of the brackets holding up the roof overhang.

Victorian period houses, possibly inspired by Japanese interiors and the large halls of English estates. Architects H. H. Richardson and McKim, Mead, and White built the most famous of these at Newport, Rhode Island. Smaller versions of the style were built in many cities around the country. The Shingle style was one of the many precursors of the American bungalow.

> THE SHINGLE STYLE WAS ONE OF THE MANY PRECURSORS OF THE AMERICAN BUNGALOW.

As in England, early bungalows in America were built as second homes at the seashore. The first house built in the United States that was actually called a bungalow was built at Monument Beach, Cape Cod, in 1879. Designed by William Gibbons Preston, a Boston architect, it didn't meet the accepted definition of a bungalow, being two and a half stories tall, and was vaguely Queen Anne in style. Nonetheless, it had a low-pitched roof, wide bargeboards, timber-like openwork in the gables, knee-braces, and double-hung windows with multi-light top sashes over one-light lower sashes, all of which became typical bungalow elements. The wraparound verandah was supported by simple posts with diagonal brackets, similar to what was used on Stick Style houses.

In 1884, New York architect Arnold W. Brunner featured a sketch of what he called a "bunga-low" (with an attic) as the fron-tispiece of the book *Cottages*. The low, T-shaped house with half-timbering in the gables was remarkably plain for a house of the time period, although it did have turned posts supporting the porch roof and turned balusters in the railings, unlike the plain posts of Gibbons's bungalow.

Other houses were built that were called "bungalows," the term at that time having more to do

Curvy half-timbering was also popular, as on this bungalow just down the street from the one on the facing page. On this home, the "timbers" are stained a more appro-priate "weathered wood" color.

2351

Half-timbering is a decorative feature of many bungalow gables, and this bungalow in Los Angeles' West Adams neighborhood is no exception. You can tell it's LA by the palm trees.

with the idea of a vacation home than with the idea of a one-
story house. As the term "cottage" was applied absurdly to the
huge mansions built by wealthy industrialists at Newport,
Rhode Island, so the term "bungalow" was applied to large,
mostly Shingle style second homes. An important aspect to a
home, whether called a "bungalow," "cottage," or "villa," was
that it was in the country, or at least surrounded by some land.
The back-to-nature trend had begun earlier in the century, and
was encouraged by plan book producers like Downing. It may
not have been a coincidence that Downing favored houses in a
country setting, since he was trained as a landscape architect.
He even encouraged growing vines on the house, which most
architects of his day would have thought ridiculous, but which
became a major tenet of bungalow landscaping later on.

The first home in the United States to be called a bungalow was built on Buzzards Bay near
the town of Bourne on Cape Cod. As with the first British bungalows, it was a vacation home,
probably for a Bostonian. Many of the details that later appeared on bungalows can be seen
on this home: the simple porch brackets, open gable decoration, asymmetrical massing, large
decorative fascia boards, multi-light upper sashes, and simple corbels. But my favorite thing
on the house is the shark fin? sea serpent? embellishment of the ridgeline.

Most heavily forested countries have a log-building tradition, and I don't know who built this log bungalow in Milwaukee, but it is a tour-de-force of log building. Just look at those log brackets! It must once have had a wood-shingle "thatch" roof as well. It just seems like one of those really special houses, kind of like the bunga-mansion, that just provokes an, "Oh, wow—I love that house!" reaction, at least for me. Unfortunately, it appears to be rather neglected. I hope someone will rescue it soon.

Though nowhere near the Adirondacks, a shingled bungalow in Memphis, Tennessee, features not only tapered columns made of stacked logs, but also log facing on the chimney and tree branches used as brackets in the gable as well as under the porch roof. By the back door on the left, a screen constructed of saplings divides the porch from the backyard. The rusticity of the logs is balanced by the delicate tracery of the window muntins in the upper floor's casement windows. Local stone forms the bases for the columns and porch.

GLOBAL INSPIRATION, INDIGENOUS STYLE

As in Britain, Americans were also going to resorts for their health. Dr. Edward Livingston Trudeau set up a health resort at Saranac Lake in New York's Adirondacks, and tourists began to arrive by rail, stagecoach, and steamboat thereafter. The back-to-nature trend generated further interest in the Adirondacks. In 1877, William West Durant, the son of a Union Pacific Railroad magnate, returned from Europe to help develop the land his father owned there. In 1877, he built Camp Pine Knot, the first of the so-called "Great Camps" of the Adirondacks. Based on the Swiss chalets he had seen in Europe, but built entirely using things found in the forests, the buildings were a rustic interpretation of Swiss architecture, using notched logs for the building, decorative twigs and saplings for balconies and railings, and local stone for chimneys and foundations. To prevent fire, he clustered the sleeping quarters in separate buildings away from the dining room and kitchen, but connected them all with decorative covered walkways. Pretty soon wealthy people were buying up large tracts of land and building their own camps, copying the style. Eventually the style spawned a chair even more iconic than the Morris chair, the Adirondack chair.

Of course, log cabins were already known in America, the

The Riordan House was built in Flagstaff, Arizona, in 1904 (before Arizona became a state) for brothers Timothy and Michael Riordan. The house contains two almost identical wings, one for each brother's family, that are connected by this communal billiard room. Though appearing to be built of logs, the home is actually frame construction covered with half-log siding and shingles. The home was designed by Charles Whittlesey, who later designed the El Tovar Hotel at the Grand Canyon. The unusual windows in the room utilize photos taken by John Hiller, the photographer for John Wesley Powell's expedition (one of my many relatives, I'm sure). The photographs are printed directly on the glass. Below the windows, a leather-upholstered Stickley bench keeps company with a wicker rocking chair. The Riordan House is now open to the public as a state park.

On the outside of the Riordan House, half-logs are used not only for siding but also for window trim. Art-glass transoms decorate the tops of the windows. Interestingly enough, most of the interior, with the exception of the billiard room, is not terribly rustic; in fact, much of it is quite delicate, having more in common with a Colonial Revival home than a rustic Arts and Crafts house.

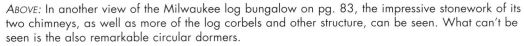

ABOVE: In another view of the Milwaukee log bungalow on pg. 83, the impressive stonework of its two chimneys, as well as more of the log corbels and other structure, can be seen. What can't be seen is the also remarkable circular dormers.

RIGHT: An extremely rustic stone porch that looks as though it could collapse at any moment supports part of the second floor of the Riordan House. Even the rafter tails make use of logs. The Riordans did own a lumber mill, and the siding makes use of parts that were cut off the logs at the mill in order to square them.

Some subtle Prairie influences show up on a gold-brick Milwaukee bungalow, particularly the cast-stone ornament of the shallow
niches on the porch columns, as well as some very nice wooden ornament in the porch gable. Apparently this home has lost its urns,
they having been replaced with square wooden planters. A set of four arched windows in the shed dormer is another unusual touch.

log-building tradition having arrived with Scandinavian, German, Swiss, and even Russian settlers. Log building was soon adopted everywhere there were lots of trees, because it could be done with the simplest of tools, an axe.

In the 1890s, houses began to appear that resembled the Anglo-Indian bungalows: hip-roofed with verandahs on one or more sides, set low to the ground. Part of the inspiration may have come from similar houses built first by the Spanish, and then by the French, in Louisiana and environs. These featured hipped roofs with swooping eaves extended over galleries or verandahs, precursor to the flared or "kicked" eaves found on many bungalows later on. Certainly covered porches make sense in a warm climate, be it India or Mississippi.

Another antecedent for the flared eaves was, of course, Japan. In 1893, Chicago hosted the World's Columbian Exposition. Though most of the buildings were in a Classical Revival style, the Japanese exhibit, called the *Ho-o-den*, was a replica of a Japanese temple. Interest in Japan had been growing tremendously in the two decades since it had

THE SHINGLE STYLE WAS ONE OF THE MANY PRECURSORS OF THE AMERICAN BUNGALOW.

begun to trade with the West. Japanese art and decorative art was already popular as part of eclectic Aesthetic interiors, which were just as popular in America as in Britain. The exhibit influenced many architects, especially the local ones, with its graceful roofline, wide eaves, timber framing, horizontal lines, and simple ornament. The flowing interior spaces also had an influence, with movable walls on both interior and exterior.

Chicago was already developing its own style of architecture as it rebuilt after the Great Fire of 1871. Known as the "Chicago School," these early steel-framed buildings were the first skyscrapers. Usually clad in masonry or terra-cotta, their minimal ornament, and more important, their distinctive three-part windows, consisting of a large, fixed pane flanked by two operable windows, were later adopted for use on bungalows. Architect William Le Baron Jenney was instrumental in the development of steel framing, and many architects who went on to greater fame started in his office, including Louis Sullivan, Daniel Burnham, John Wellborn Root, and William Holabird.

Sullivan went on to mentor many of the young architects who eventually formed what became known as the Prairie School. Sullivan's style of luxuriant organic ornament

ABOVE: I might as well admit my weakness for Prairie houses right up front. I think maybe it's the four-foot overhangs. Anyway, here's the 1902 Heurtley House, a Prairie house by the most famous of the Prairie School architects, Frank Lloyd Wright. This Oak Park, Illinois, home still looks very modern, so one can only imagine how shocking it was in 1902. It has the usual "Where the hell is the front door?" mystery of most of Wright's Prairie houses—he called it "the path of discovery."

RIGHT: The Prairie influence on this home is the off-center hip-roof dormer, whose roof has deep overhangs entirely out of scale with the rest of it, dwarfing its three square windows. The porch roof, only partly seen, has a similar out-of-scale quality. And, of course, it has a shallow footed urn, which no self-respecting Prairie house would be without.

was clearly influenced by Arts and Crafts as well as Art Nouveau. The most well-known architects of the Prairie School included Frank Lloyd Wright, George Washington Maher, Walter Burley Griffin and his wife Marion Mahoney, George Elmslie, William Gray Purcell, George Feick, and William S. Drummond. Besides the influence of Sullivan, they would certainly have been aware of the Arts and Crafts Movement, the Chicago Arts and Crafts Society having been formed in 1898. Shortly after the Columbian Exposition, houses that are clearly influenced by the Japanese buildings begin to appear. Wide overhanging eaves (usually boxed in), flat planes of brick or

A Prairie house doesn't have to be square, as proved here by Memphis architect Neander Woods. Nor does it have to have consistent rooflines. It can be X-shaped instead, like this home. Rooms jut out every which way, taking advantage of the corner lot. Massive limestone columns support a second-floor porch covered by a hipped roof, while to the right of it a gabled roof shelters another room with a rounded, flat-roofed bay protruding from the front. A clipped gable dormer caps the whole thing, and the variety of muntin patterns only adds to the zaniness.

ABOVE: It's easy to see how the Prairie School influenced the later Chicago bungalows, with casement windows (often with stylized geometric art glass), square columns, flat enclosed eaves (although the bungalow in the foreground has gotten the unfortunate aluminum soffit replacement), and the all-important urns on the porch. It is not true that Chicago ordinance requires urns to be planted only with red geraniums—this one appears to have blue salvia instead.

RIGHT: One of the hallmarks of the Prairie style is banded, or ribbon, casement windows—that is, three or more casement windows in a row. These ribbon windows added to the horizontality embraced by Prairie School architects. This home, though rather taller than the average Chicago-style bungalow, nonetheless retains the brick with limestone detailing, planter box brackets (the box is missing, as usual), and small porch that are typical.

stucco accented by flat horizontal and vertical wood trim, and bands of art glass windows were the hallmarks of the Prairie style. Most Prairie style houses were two stories and therefore not really bungalows, but the wide eaves, often hipped roofs, generally horizontal aspect, and art glass windows were later adapted for bungalows.

There's a certain monumental quality to Prairie houses, like this Milwaukee example. Built of the thin Roman brick also favored by Wright, the sloping sides and minimal detailing (only some concrete horizontal bands on the second floor and another band of decorative brick just below the overhang) still give it a sense of presence on the street.

A very handsome Prairie-style duplex in Milwaukee utilizes wire-cut brick and stucco, the stucco of the upper story being subtly recessed from the top of the brick.
Notice how the moldings under the eaves work into the design. The upper floor
has an enclosed sun porch that comes out to the edge of the eaves, emphasizing
the recessed area over the arched front door.

Big overhangs, a roof that appears flat (though often they aren't quite), lots of horizontal lines, front door not immediately obvious—yup, it's a Prairie house. A canti-levered balcony doesn't hurt, either. And being in Oak Park, how could it help it?

POPCORN AND CAPITALISM

But it was in California that the bungalow reached its full potential, in a fascinating confluence of myth and capitalism, mass migration, high art and popular taste. In California, the philosophy of the Arts and Crafts Movement, combined with democratic ideals and a typically American practicality, finally accomplished at least part of what the British founders had hoped for—artistic homes for nearly everyone.

Probably this would not have happened except for two things. The first was the Gold Rush of 1849, which brought half a million people to California in search of instant wealth, and the Transcontinental Railroad, completed in 1869 (with later connections to Los Angeles in 1887), which made it easier to get there.

A brief digression regarding the Transcontinental Railroad: History is always written by the victors, which is why the Transcontinental Railroad is widely regarded as the brainchild of The Big Four—Collis P. Huntington, Leland Stanford, Mark Hopkins, and Charles Crocker. It was in fact the lifelong dream of an engineer, Theodore M. Judah, who not only mapped out the route for the western half of the railroad, rounded up the investors (the previously mentioned Big Four), and lobbied Congress for approval. He was eventually shut out by the investors, and died in 1863 before the railroad was completed. The Big Four took most of the credit, though Judah does have a street named after him in San Francisco.

Stone, brick, wood, shingles, open porches, shallowly pitched roofs with deep overhangs, and, of course, palm trees—this Pasadena home has many of the characteristics that have come to be associated with California bungalows.

The Gold Rush and the railroad turned San Francisco from a tiny settlement into a great city in only a few decades. By 1880, it had a population of 250,000. By comparison, the population of Los Angeles in 1880 was 15,000, though that was to change when the railroad arrived there in 1887. The railroads changed the duration of a cross-country trip from a few

months to a few days. People from the East and Midwest began to immigrate to California, and wealthy people began to vacation in California to avoid the cold winters back home. The railroads naturally encouraged this sort of thing, and books, magazines, and periodicals waxed rhapsodic about the mild winters, year-round flowers, and healthful air to be found in California.

ABOVE: Postcards of bungalows covered in flowers and vines, and, of course, the ubiquitous palm trees (although orange groves were popular as well), and nearly always labeled with some variation of "California bungalows in Winter" probably persuaded many a chilly easterner to move here. I can still remember my mother being astounded when we first moved here from the Midwest at the banks covered with geraniums or nasturtiums essentially growing wild. I still get a certain thrill from walking out into my backyard and picking a lemon whenever I want one, even though I've lived here over forty years now.

RIGHT: Without a whole lot of guilt, proselytizers for the Arts and Crafts Movement recommended Native American rugs, blankets, baskets, and pottery as part of appropriate bungalow décor, and many owners embraced this wholeheartedly. In a Berkeley living room, a Gustav Stickley settle and a Limbert rocker complement Navajo rugs from the teens and twenties. A painting by William Keith, whose paintings are an integral part of the Swedenborgian Church in San Francisco, hangs over the settle. French doors on the right lead to the entry hall, while the ones on the left open to a step-down study. The woodwork is dark-stained Douglas fir, found in a great majority of northern California bungalows.

There were those, though, who didn't think much of San Francisco's nineteenth-century architecture, of which the city is now so proud. Fred T. Hodgson wrote in the preface to his *Practical Cottages and Bungalows* in 1906, "With San Francisco and some of the other cities in mind, it may sound extravagant to say that Californians have any advantage of any kind in the way of an architectural tradition. Assuredly, the old wooden dwelling in San Francisco was the worst type of residence ever built in large numbers in any city in the world. It possessed, we believe, every known and conceivable architectural demerit, and the city in which these sinful disorders were committed can never be completely reformed save by a sort of architectural vigilance committee." Oh, come on, Fred, tell us what you really think.

The state had already been named after a myth, which

described an island ruled by beautiful Amazons that was a "terrestrial paradise", where gold and precious gems lay on the ground just waiting to be picked up. (They apparently wanted to ignore the other part of the myth—that these women killed any man who dared to set foot on the island and fed him to the griffons they used as steeds.) The myth fed the Gold Rush, and the 1884 novel, *Ramona*, by Helen Hunt Jackson, fed the myth. The book, meant to illustrate the plight of California's Native Americans, instead was embraced for its romantic view of the life of the *Californios*, the descendants of the original Spanish land grant owners, and only added to the myth, especially in Southern California.

San Francisco put on its own exposition in 1894, the California Midwinter International Exposition. It featured a Japanese exhibit—an entire acre of Japanese gardens and buildings—sponsored by George Turner Marsh, who in 1876 had opened the first shop in America devoted to Japanese art, which was located in the Palace Hotel in San Francisco. (Large parts of the exhibit have been preserved as the Japanese Tea Garden in San Francisco's Golden Gate Park.) As in Chicago, the exposition influenced local architecture.

There was wealth in California, not only the fortunes made in the Gold Rush but also others made in mining, agriculture, and, of course, land speculation. The influx of people meant there was a great deal of building going on, and this naturally attracted architects, most of whom came from the East and the Midwest; some of these architects included Bernard Maybeck, A. Page Brown, A.C. Schweinfurth, Willis Polk, Charles and Henry Greene, Ernest Coxhead, Myron Hunt, Elmer Grey, and Irving Gill.

> IT IS GENERALLY AGREED THAT JOSEPH WORCESTER'S HOUSE, BUILT IN 1876 ACROSS THE BAY FROM SAN FRANCISCO IN PIEDMONT, WAS THE FIRST ARTS AND CRAFTS HOUSE IN CALIFORNIA.

A atrium with a fountain forms the core of the Duncan-Irwin House by Greene and Greene. Although partly a response to the limitations of trying to remodel the existing Duncan home for new owner Theodore Irwin, it is nonetheless a lovely sunlit outdoor space that can be accessed by French doors from several different downstairs rooms, while upstairs, open walkways link the various bedrooms and other rooms of the second floor. In many ways the plan is reminiscent of the Spanish colonial buildings found in California that were romanticized in the novel *Ramona*.

It is generally agreed that Joseph Worcester's house, built in 1876 across the Bay from San Francisco in Piedmont, was the first Arts and Crafts house in California. Worcester was a Swedenborgian minister who had come from New England to the West for his health. He had considered becoming an architect before taking up the ministry, and was an admirer of the writings of Thoreau, Emerson, and Ruskin. He was also a friend of the naturalist John Muir, and they both shared a reverential view of nature. He designed his own house, which was rustic

A stone foundation and chimney pairs with roughcast stucco and half-timbering on a Berkeley bungalow. Typically the exterior wood was stained rather than painted.

and reflected his ideals of harmony with nature. He designed two other houses on Russian Hill in San Francisco, but when it came time to design the church for his new congregation, he hired A. Page Brown. Did he ever get to be THE Page Brown? (It is likely the church was actually designed by Bernard Maybeck and A.C. Schweinfurth, who were both working in Brown's office at the time.) The church was (and is) quite rustic, and according to legend, Worcester actually went to the Santa Cruz Mountains to personally select the madrone trees that hold up its roof.

Meanwhile, in Southern California, architects like Charles and Henry Greene, the brothers Arthur and Alfred Heineman, Louis B. Easton, Irving Gill, and Myron Hunt and Elmer Grey were experimenting with a similar rustic style.

Arroyo stone piers and stained-shingle siding surround a welcoming front porch on an Eagle Rock, California, bungalow. The north-facing front yard is landscaped with shade-loving plants like ferns and calla lilies.

The setting sun illuminates the porch gable and matching dormer of another Eagle Rock bungalow. Bevel siding, doubled wooden pillars, and an oak front door with art-glass panes above a corbeled shelf form a simple yet artistic facade.

The bungalow court was invented in southern California by Arthur and Alfred Heineman, who later went on to design the country's first motel, based on a similar model. Small bungalows around a central courtyard is still a pretty civilized way to live. This bungalow court in Pasadena mixes one- and two-story buildings of varying designs into a cohesive whole. Parking is in the back, as it should be.

THE IDEAL HOME

Arts and Crafts ideals had begun to spread across America in the late nineteenth century. The furnishings had become fashionable (though often without the ideals attached) and promoted in periodicals like *Ladies Home Journal* and *House Beautiful*. Around the turn of the century, others including Gustav Stickley's *Craftsman* and Elbert Hubbard's *The Fra and The Philistine* joined these magazines. There were also building magazines like *Keith's*. Arts and Crafts societies and clubs were established in major cities. The pieces were in place, the influences absorbed.

No one really knows what caused bungalows to start being built in California. It's kind of like making popcorn—nothing happens, then one kernel pops, then another, and another, then a few at a time, then they all start popping at once. Was it the mild climate? Certainly the bungalow was appropriate for a warm climate, and having no need to dig a basement made them cheaper to build. Was it the availability of wood from redwood and Douglas fir forests? Probably didn't hurt. Was it the cheap land? Maybe, but land was cheap in a lot of places. Was it the demand for housing? Partly. Was it capitalism at work? Unquestionably. Was it Arts and Crafts ideals manifested as houses? Absolutely.

But that wasn't all of it. There was something special about California, partly myth, partly reality. It's always been the Promised Land, all the way back to the original myth. It was still the frontier. People came here to have different lives than they could have elsewhere. There was a certain optimism and willingness to try new things. Bungalows were a new thing, and they seemed to fit somehow. By the turn of the twentieth century, the bungalow boom in California had begun.

Although many bungalows were designed by known architects, included those mentioned above, the great majority of them weren't. The simplicity of the style lent itself to endless variations of the basic elements, and soon individual builders, building companies, and land speculators were throwing up tracts of bungalows. Plan books, already a fixture since the nineteenth century, began to feature bungalows. Anonymous architects or delineators designed most of these, though not all.

The hope of plan book publishers was that people would buy the actual plans from them at a price generally somewhere between five to twenty-five dollars, yet plan books

Spreading, shallowly pitched roofs with brackets, a pop-top, and an arroyo-stone foundation combine with an interesting beveled siding pattern on an Eagle Rock, California, bungalow.

RIGHT: A cantilevered, clipped gable over the arched double entry doors of the Women's Twentieth Century Club in Eagle Rock mirrors the larger gable that spreads over the rest of the building. Many clubs of this sort, with an Arts and Crafts orientation, were set up in the early years of the twentieth century in many cities across the United States.

OPPOSITE PAGE: The influence of Greene and Greene is everywhere in Pasadena, showing up here in the front door's art glass and sidelights, and in what I consider to be the universal Pasadena bungalow window—a casement divided one-third/two-thirds by a single horizontal muntin, with a top casing that extends considerably beyond the side casings.

were usually given away or sold more cheaply. Some were nothing more than a black-and-white catalog, while others were lushly illustrated in color. There was usually a photo or illustration of each house accompanied by a simplified floor plan, and often a lot of purple prose describing the house. For example, this 1920s Henry L. Wilson Company catalog stated: "Here is a little gem that will appeal to every lover of inexpensive, artistic homes. Its irregular but harmonious lines will at once win a place in the heart of seekers of something pleasing. This bungalow does not cost any more, but it 'looks like more' and that is what most of us want, our money's worth; and for a comfortable, homelike bungalow to fit the ordinary purse it has few equals and no superiors. Cleverly arranged and indicative of ability in artistic designing this bungalow speaks for itself." (Although if the bungalow spoke for itself, perhaps it would make more sense than Mr. Wilson, who called his catalog: *A Short Sketch of the Evolution of the Bungalow: From its Primitive Crudeness to its present state of Artistic Beauty.*)

There were many plan books and mail order house books, published by architects, lumber companies, builders, real estate syndicates, and, of course, the national mail order companies Sears Roebuck and Montgomery Ward. Gustav Stickley's *Craftsman* magazine also published two plan books of designs. No doubt there were people who

This is the quintessential southern California pier: stones and concrete topped by an art-glass lantern with the same spreading roof and wide eaves as the bungalow it accompanies.

just took the photo and floor plan to a builder and had it copied, or builders who built from plan books without actually purchasing the plans. There is also evidence that many of the plan book publishers copied the designs of well-known architects and published them as their own, maybe with slight alterations.

By the early twentieth century, there were probably hundreds of plan books, including Gustav Stickley's *Craftsman* magazine and *More Craftsman Homes*, which featured houses taken from the pages of the magazine. Other plan books available at the time included: *Our Book of Attractive Small Homes* by the Beatty Lumber Company of Morris, Illinois; *Central's Book of Homes* by the Central Lumber Company of Reading, Pennsylvania; *Radford's Artistic Bungalows* by the Radford Architectural Company of Chicago, Illinois; *California Homes*

A hillside bungalow like this one in Seattle probably didn't come from a plan book, but a plan book may have served as inspiration for the designer. Clinker bricks, half-timbered stucco, and shingles (on the dormer to the right of the main gable) cover the house, while the piers and railings combine stone and bricks, and the off-center steps leading to the porch add to the artistic effect. Because of the steep hillside site, the front yard is terraced with several levels of stone retaining walls.

The twin gables of this bungalow in Denver sport some interesting ornamental wooden doo-dads against the rough stucco. The part gable/part pergola porch is a typical feature on many bungalows. What sets this one apart is the clinker brick and stone "peanut brittle" masonry of the porch piers and railing: look carefully at some of the reddish "stones," as they are actually extremely misshapen clinker bricks. One of the reasons bungalow designers embraced clinker bricks is because of their interesting shapes and colors. Well, that and the fact that they were cheap.

Book of Houseplans by Dixon and Hillen of Oakland, California; *Loizeaux's Plan Book No. 7* by the Loizeaux Lumber Company of Plainfield, New Jersey; *Building With Assurance* by the Morgan Woodwork Organization of Chicago, Illinois; *One Hundred Bungalows* by the Building Brick Association of America in Boston, Massachusetts; *Artistic Homes* by Herbert Chivers of St. Louis, Missouri; *Attractive Homes* by J.W. Lindstrom of Minneapolis, Minnesota; *Little Bungalows* by Stillwell and Company of Los Angeles, California; *The Bungalow Book* by Charles E. White, Jr. of New York; *Artistic Bungalows* by the Architectural Construction Company, *Allen Bungalows* by the W.E. Allen Company, *The Bungalow Book* by the Standard Building and Investment Company, and *Bungalows* by Edward E. Sweet, all of Los Angeles; Harris Bros. of Chicago, Illinois; as well as plan books by The Bungalowcraft Company, Ye Planry, Stillwell and Company, of Los Angeles, California; The Craftsman Bungalow Company and the Long Building Company of Seattle, Washington; Harris Bros. of Chicago, Illinois, and the aforementioned Henry L. Wilson, who called himself the "Bungalow Man." Wilson also published *Bungalow Magazine* from 1907 to 1912. In 1912 he sold it to Jud Yoho of the Craftsman Bungalow Company in Seattle, where it continued to be published until 1916. It's interesting to note that many of the plan books, especially the ones offered by lumber companies, offer exactly the same models. Possibly there were architectural companies that just offered their plans to lumberyards and allowed them to put their own names on them, no doubt in exchange for a percentage of sales. Ah, capitalism at work.

Land speculators would often subdivide land and sell the lots, allowing the new owners to choose a builder or an architect on their own, while others offered the entire package. Smaller builders would buy only a few lots, and on many streets in many California cities you can find a row of four or five houses all by the same builder, though unlike modern tract homes they are not all the same, rather, each would have different details such as window muntins, roof shape, shape of pillars, differing front door style, etc., though usually the same floor plan. Varying built-ins, colonnades, fireplaces, light fixtures, and so forth would also differentiate the interiors.

After the Great Earthquake and Fire in San Francisco in 1906, the building boom reached a frenzied pace in Northern California. Many of the San Francisco refugees had come to Berkeley and Oakland and other cities across the Bay and decided to stay there.

Three-car garages were not the norm for bungalows, though there were probably a few. A one-car garage was far more likely, and these were almost always detached. Even a three-car garage would have had individual bays, as this garage in Pasadena displays. The taller bay (this being a new garage) is probably for an RV.

The warm climate in Florida also lent itself to California-style bungalows. A postcard of the Arlington Terrace development in St. Petersburg shows bungalows that are almost identical to their California counterparts. Besides the lovely piers that mark the street entrance to the development, with their built-in planters, the photograph shows two cars, one in the foreground and one parked down the street at the far right side of the photo. I'm not an expert on cars so I don't know what year this might have been taken. The truly remarkable thing, if one looks closely, is that a woman is driving and a man is sitting in the passenger seat—an unlikely scenario at the time.

Arlington Terrace, a Bungalow Vista, St. Petersburg, Fla.—37

The porte cochere, which in earlier centuries allowed residents and guests to alight from carriages out of the weather, easily adapted to a new form of transportation, the automobile. Of all the cities we visited, Memphis had more porte cocheres on bungalows than any other. Even the most unassuming bungalows were equipped with porte cocheres. This particular home is not at all unassuming, with its pediment-like porch gable, and a port cochere supported on three muscular brick-and-limestone pillars with oversized wooden capitals. Unfortunately, the pillars on many porte cocheres in many cities have been replaced with four-by-fours or metal pipe columns to accommodate larger cars, trucks, and sport utility vehicles.

The building of the University of California in Berkeley also attracted many new residents.

The idea of the bungalow as a single family house on its own plot of land would probably not have been possible without the advent of both streetcars and automobiles. Bungalows were primarily built in the new "streetcar suburbs" that soon surrounded the urban core of many cities, not just those in California. As automobiles became more popular, bungalow tracts accommodated them with garages.

FREEDOM OF ASSEMBLY

As bungalows blossomed in California, the plan books, and soon, the ready-cut house companies, brought the bungalow idea to the rest of the country. Sears Roebuck published their first book of house plans in 1908, and would also supply almost everything necessary to build the house. A few years later they began to offer ready-cut home kits. They were not the first company to offer pre-cut buildings—that honor goes to the Aladdin Company of Bay City, Michigan, which offered its first pre-cut building, a boathouse, in 1906. By the 'teens, the company was publishing a hundred-page catalog of bungalows and other house styles, as well as garages, barns, and even small apartment buildings.

Other ready-cut companies followed suit, such as Lewis Homes and Sterling Homes, also of Bay City; Bennett Homes of North Tonawanda, New York; Gordon Van-Tine Homes of Davenport, Iowa: California Ready-Cut Bungalows and Pacific Ready-Cut Homes of Los Angeles, California; Robinson's Money-Saving Mill-Made Cut-to-Fit Houses of Providence, Rhode Island (a real tongue-twister, and a little hyphen-happy to boot); Ready-Built House Company and The Rice-Penne Company of Portland, Oregon; The Ainslie-Boyd Company of Seattle, Washington; and the Thayer Portable

House Company of Keene, New Hampshire. There were probably others even more obscure than some of these.

Obviously pre-cut buildings were totally at odds with the Arts and Crafts ideal of hand-craftsmanship. Most of the companies actually touted their machinery, explaining how it could cut lumber more economically and with less waste. Pre-cut buildings were also marketed as a do-it-yourself proposition—that any man (and it was always men)

ABOVE: Multiple gables combine with a flat-roofed porch on a stucco bungalow with stone and brick detailing. The chimney, built of local stone, shows some flair with its crenellated top. I'm pretty sure this bungalow is in New Jersey.

LEFT: This very tall Milwaukee bungalow shows how the essential details could adapt to local conditions (steeper roof, smaller porch) while maintaining the bungalow style (fancy purlins, multiple timber columns, massive piers, and exposed rafters). The stone of the porch may or may not be original to the home.

Local stone, multicolored brick and half-timbered stucco combine on a simple cross-gabled bungalow in Memphis. Gold-colored bricks were less common in Memphis, where red brick combined with limestone were the building materials of choice.

Unusual diamond-shaped windows decorate the half-timbered dormer of a plan book bungalow in Victoria, B.C. Dentil molding, a classical detail, is far more common on bungalows than one might suspect. Architectural purity was not common with plan book designers. Do I have to say that yellow and white is not really an appropriate color combination for a bungalow? Think earth tones. Think unpainted shingles.

Clipped gables and arched windows were popular in Milwaukee (and elsewhere). On this home, the porch has been glassed-in, a common modification in colder climates (though I'm not saying it's the right thing to do).

who knew how to swing a hammer could assemble the pre-cut, carefully numbered parts into a house. It was this practicality and willingness to use machinery that allowed not only the houses, but also many of the decorative objects associated with the American Arts and Crafts Movement to actually be affordable not only to the middle class, but also to the working class, as the original founders of the British movement had hoped for.

Most of these bungalows lacked the refined sensibilities of Arts and Crafts homes designed by architects like Charles and Henry Greene or Frank Lloyd Wright. Nonetheless, it is remarkable how many of the ideas that came to typify the American Arts and Crafts Movement filtered down into the basic tract bungalow.

Because America had no medieval tradition to look back to, the Arts and Crafts Movement in America looked instead to homegrown precedents—the simple saltbox houses of New England, log buildings, the Spanish buildings of California and the Southwest, vernacular houses of all kinds. Then they added influences from outside: Japanese, Swiss, Scandinavian, German, English. They embraced wooden construction and the use of local materials. And they embraced simplicity, artistry, hominess, rusticity, and nature. They were, and are, a distinctly American style house, unlike anything built before or since.

> IT IS REMARKABLE HOW MANY OF THE IDEAS THAT CAME TO TYPIFY THE AMERICAN ARTS AND CRAFTS MOVEMENT FILTERED DOWN INTO THE BASIC TRACT BUNGALOW.

Soon "California bungalows" were being built all over the country, thanks to plan books and pre-cut houses. It was kind of like getting a vacation home in the city. They were altered to fit other climates: steeper roofs, enclosed porches, basements, brick walls instead of wood siding. Almost any city or town that saw growth during the early twentieth century will have bungalows. They were popular, they were fashionable, they were trendy.

The bungalow had a way of making a virtue of simplicity, informality, ease of construction, and cheapness. The word *cheap* at the time did not have the negative connotations it has today. (Retail salespeople are taught, if a customer asks for something cheaper, to say, "Our *less expensive* items are over here.") Open floor plans made the bungalow's small size seem larger, numerous pieces of built-in furniture not only saved floor space, but meant the owners didn't have to purchase furniture, the interplay of indoor and outdoor space and the addition of rooms with no specific function, or usable attic space that could be developed later, made the bungalow more flexible than other housing types. The

Those who could afford hand-craftsmanship could hire architect Henry Greene and his band of craftsmen, led by Peter and John Hall. The Gould House in Ventura, California, designed after the dissolution of Henry's partnership with his brother Charles, was a simple farmhouse that retains many of the hand-crafted touches for which Greene and Greene were known, such as art glass and exposed mortise-and-tenon joinery. Nonetheless, even this "hand-crafting" probably involved power tools.

ABOVE: Departing somewhat from the usual because of its double lot, the porte cochere on this Memphis bungalow is angled. Limestone piers support tapered wooden columns with capitals that are way too big for them, and the roof sprouts two small gable dormers.

RIGHT: Clinker bricks in the hands of skilled designers and a good mason could be extremely artistic, as amply demonstrated here in the chimney of the Duncan-Irwin House in Pasadena. They were often combined with regular bricks, river rock, other kinds of stone, or even stucco.

The rusticity of stone combined with brick was favored by bungalow designers, as shown here in these walls and benches surrounding a modern spa.

Clinker bricks were initially used because they were cheap—they were usually thrown away because they were misshapen from being too close to the fire and were thought to be unusable. But the Arts and Crafts designers liked their irregularities and improbable shapes, and they soon went from being a cheap building material to being all the rage, leading some brick companies to produce them on purpose.

In Memphis, limestone columns with oversized wooden capitals and a low wooden railing with substantial four-inch-square uprights give a monumental quality to the porch of this bungalow. Beefy beams take up the load above the pillars, and a wide fascia with unusual cutouts near the ends ornaments the latticed gable. The overscaling of elements (far more than is really needed to support this porch roof) is one of the major features of bungalows, at least in North America.

Green-stained shingles contrast with granite piers on the open porch of a bungalow in Victoria, B.C. Unlike many bungalows, this one is oriented toward the back rather than the front, as it is on a large lot overlooking the water and somewhat hidden from the street. The porch on the back side is covered and wraps around two sides of the house.

A corner lot allows a Milwaukee bungalow to show off a lot more detail, including this very large dormer with an accompanying upstairs porch. The two-tone brickwork is echoed by the two colors of the purlins and their scrolled corbels. Note the slightly upswept ridgeline at the gables.

The same kind of overscaled features, here rendered in wood, support the porch gable of a British Columbian bungalow. The tapered elephantine piers are a defining feature of many bungalows. Knee braces that appear to "pierce" the fascia board are also extremely common. It's the way in which these common elements are combined that makes each bungalow unique—in this case, an X-shaped porch railing rather than the more usual uprights.

Three leaded-glass casements increase in width as they diminish in height on the front of a Berkeley bungalow. Bevel siding on the lower portion of the home combines with shingles laid in alternating wide and narrow exposures on the upper portion, and doubled knee braces support the gable overhang.

Dark burgundy bricks and red sandstone combine with a green tile roof on a Denver bungalow. Decorative patterning in the brick, especially on the columns and around the windows, adds interest to the front façade. The open part of the porch is stepped up from the main part that is sheltered by the gable, and surrounded by a pierced brick railing capped with slabs of sandstone.

This tiny example in British Columbia sports leaded-glass windows and somewhat diminutive tapered columns covered in stucco. Equally scaled-down knee braces support its clipped porch gable. And it illustrates one of my pet peeves: if you're going to have shutters, *they must be big enough that they would actually cover the window if closed.*

Not many bungalows have towers, but this one in Milwaukee does. In fact, there's a row of three bungalows with towers. This one retains its original (and rather unusual) front door. Subtle cast-stone accents are set into the brickwork over the windows and doors, as well as a few other places, and the brickwork itself is accented by two bands of vertical bricks, one just above the windows and the other about two feet above the ground. The brick itself is cross-hatched, giving a delicate texture to the walls.

Arts and Crafts idea of allowing materials to be celebrated for what they were had the added bonus of keeping costs down.

Bungalows were also the first houses available to the masses that were truly modern, in the sense that we would think of as modern, in that they had indoor plumbing, central heat, electricity—all the modern conveniences. But there was more to bungalows than that. The Arts and Crafts advocates believed that design could change people's lives. They believed that the design of objects mattered, they believed that the built environment mattered, and they believed that people living in these houses, having these objects, raising their children there, would result in a wholesome life, upstanding citizens, and a peaceful and prosperous country.

The real heyday of bungalows lasted from the turn of the

> THE ARTS AND CRAFTS ADVOCATES BELIEVED THAT DESIGN COULD CHANGE PEOPLE'S LIVES.

20th century until the end of World War I, pretty much corresponding to the demise of the Arts and Crafts Movement (generally thought to be over with Gustav Stickley's bankruptcy in 1916 and Elbert Hubbard's death on the *Lusitania* in 1915). After the war, bungalows continued to be built, but in a much simplified style, and the growing popularity of the Romantic Revival styles (Tudor, Normandy, Spanish) cut into their popularity. Nonetheless, bungalows continued to be built well into the 1930s, though by that time they were no longer trendy. Yet the plan books and pre-cut house companies continued to offer them even as their popularity declined. (In a similar vein, ranch houses continue to be built, long after *their* heyday in the 1950s and 1960s.) There were bungalows built after 1930, and in fact the National Park Service maintained the style for park buildings long after the Arts and Crafts era was technically over.

A fairly plain bungalow of rough-cut red brick and limestone with plain stucco gables probably dates to the 1920s. For the most part, bungalows in the twenties were much simpler and had lost a lot of the rustic, hand-crafted qualities of the earlier homes. Being in Memphis, though, it still has a porte cochere.

These two Memphis bungalows are identical except for the detailing— brick columns on one, stone on the other; slightly different half-timbering on each. In bungalow neighborhoods, there will often be a whole row of bungalows by the same builder which will be differentiated only by siding materials, roof shapes, muntin patterns, porch railings, and so forth.

Probably because of the overscaled nature of many of their components, bungalows seem remarkably solid and sturdy, and that seemed to somehow go along with the idea that living in these houses would produce levelheaded and reliable citizens. If only that were all it took, we'd be in business. But I don't discount the influence of the built environment entirely. In the era we are living in now, where most things are flimsy and disposable, how will our children learn to value anything or care for it, whether that be material objects, relationships, or the community at large? At the very least, the massive limestone columns on this Memphis bungalow will not dent when accidentally bumped into, unlike the synthetic stucco over styrofoam so popular in modern tract houses.

ABOVE: Dentil molding trims not only the bottom of the gable but also the tops of the tapered columns on a raised-basement bungalow in Vancouver, B.C. Raised basements are often used in climates where real basements aren't required, because it gives the equivalent of a basement, or at least a crawl space that you don't actually have to crawl in.

LEFT: Not one but three Chicago windows with an unusual curved muntin in the center window adorn the front of a stucco-and-bevel-sided bungalow in British Columbia. Six rather large brackets are apparently required to hold up the beam over the front door, and an additional three each for the window boxes. Well, wet dirt IS heavy.

RIGHT: While still within bungalow parameters, this Memphis home is definitely heading in several other directions. The low-pitched roof, exposed rafters, and large pillars of the front porch are comfortably bungalow-like, and even an octagonal bay is not unheard of on a bungalow, but the almost nonexistent overhangs on some parts of it are heading toward Romantic Revival styles like Normandy and Tudor.

BELOW: Bungalow designers certainly took delight in what they could do with the form, even in the 1920s as bungalows began to become simplified. The Samuels House in Memphis, designed by Mahan and Broadwell in 1922, is a festival of green-tiled rooflines, asymmetrical massing, and interesting ornament. Apparently not only were twelve purlins required to hold up the overhang of the porch gable, but the two-foot-square pillars underneath were not adequate and had to be supplemented by four twisted columns that had wandered over from some Spanish revival house around the corner. The ornament that decorates the gables is of unknown architectural parentage. And it *is* Memphis, so, of course, there's a porte cochere.

These may not be the biggest pillars I've ever seen, but they're definitely in the top ten. And nothing screams "bungalow" like a humongous pillar. There's a certain Prairie influence on this Memphis home as well, with the boxed-in eaves and architectural restraint. Okay, I'm using the term architectural restraint very loosely.

ICON AND IRONY

There are those who deem the Arts and Crafts Movement, both in Britain and America, to have been a failure. A recurring joke among people in what is now being called the Arts and Crafts Revival (sparked by the 1972 Arts and Crafts Exhibition at Princeton) is that the revival has now lasted longer than the original movement. In part, the movement was doomed to fail, as any such movement is probably doomed to fail in the face of corporate capitalism. Yet Britain adopted many of the ideas first put forth by the Socialists, including a few we ought to adopt here, like the National Health and six weeks vacation. William Morris designs are still in production, and though he might not have liked it, now available to the masses as notecards and wrapping paper, courtesy of machine printing processes. In America, bungalows have become popular again, because they still work for 21st century life, and unlike modern houses with three inch MDF (medium-density fiberboard) baseboards and spray textured sheetrock, bungalows are solidly built using a quality of materials that is no longer available except to the wealthy. And the popularity of the Revival means that items of Arts and Crafts design, even if they are not infused with the ideals of the movement, are nonetheless available to nearly everyone.

For the bungalow–the very symbol of British colonialism (some would say imperialism)—to become the icon of a Progressive design movement in America is ironic to say the least. It is true that by the time other influences were added, the American bungalow had become different than its Indian antecedents, leaving only the one-story form and low-pitched roof as an indicator of its origins. It's unlikely that the first bungalow enthusiasts recognized the irony at that time—only hindsight allows us to do so now. Nonetheless, we took the form and made it our own, and made it a symbol of democratic values and artistic ideals. That bungalows are still remarkably suited to 21st-century life says much for their design, and much for the movement that gave rise to them.

Still don't understand? Perhaps you have not yet reached bungalow *satori*. Meditate on this koan:

Q. If a Zen Buddhist is rolling downhill on all four wheels, how many pancakes does it take to cover a bungalow?

A. Catsup.

Though the woodwork has been painted, the baseboards are still six inches high, the door casings are still five inches wide, the doors are really wood, not veneered hardboard, and the walls are made of real plaster, not drywall. The picture molding dividing the wall allows for two different colors as well as a decorative stencil border. On the oak sideboard, a collection of art pottery is set off by the warm tones of the wood.

ABOVE: Unlike bungalows in India, but very much like bungalows in Denver, this small home has subtle detailing in the brick: a band just under the window box stands slightly proud of the wall surface, and some decorative brickwork also protrudes slightly from the pillars (which are humongous, as usual). A tripartite window features stained glass in the center portion. A low brick planter box has been constructed across the entire front of the home.

RIGHT: Bungalows like this one in midtown Memphis are becoming desirable places to live again. The reasons the original owners bought bungalows (artistic design, informal lifestyle, modern conveniences, proximity to transportation) are the same for a new generation of owners. The popularity of the Arts and Crafts revival, while diluting its purity for some, has nonetheless opened the eyes of people who might not otherwise have known the joy of bungalows. The bungalows' simplicity and open floor plans make them easily adaptable to twenty-first-century life.

No style of bungalow was more popular than the side-gabled version with a dormer. A classic example of the genre—with tapered piers, structural-looking "pierced" timber pillars, two kinds of siding, a Chicago window with transoms, and three knee braces in the gable—it is still set apart from its neighbors by the diamond-shaped muntins in the dormer windows and the atypical latticework under the porch. Though this bungalow is in British Columbia, its brethren can be found in every city that grew rapidly in the early twentieth century.

A little tall to really be considered a bungalow, this home in British Columbia has all the details any bungalow could ask for—a bit too many, maybe. Brackets? We got 'em—under the window boxes, under the protruding gable ends, under the overhanging second floor, under the window hoods—perhaps there was a sale on brackets at the lumberyard that day. Slightly bulbous Tuscan columns with oversize capitals? Check. Stone porch foundation? Absolutely. Art glass in the window transoms? Got that covered. Inappropriate white trim? Unfortunately.

ABOVE: The curving ridgelines and tile roof of this Memphis bungalow would have been right at home in India, but it all goes haywire from there. Lovely zig-zaggy corbels support the overhang, and a larger version of the same flanks the flattened arch of the porch roof. Meanwhile, lots of diamond-shaped ornament decorates the brickwork. Throw in a little dentil molding and a Palladian window in the Dutch gable and what do you have? You still have a bungalow.

RIGHT: An interplay of siding, shingles, and tapered brick piers form an inviting front porch for a Seattle bungalow. The gable overhang features characteristic fake purlins.

ABOVE: A very California-looking bungalow somehow landed in this Memphis neighborhood. It has an interesting wood siding pattern of narrow bevel siding interspersed with wider boards in the gable. Note that the shutters flanking the front door's sidelights *are* actually big enough for a change. These people obviously have a total red-and-white theme going, right down to the azaleas.

RIGHT: An enclosed porch, clipped gables, beige brick—could this be Milwaukee? Insets of stone in the brick make for a more interesting façade, and the battered (slanted) sides of the porch give it a certain solidity. A proper wooden storm door protects the front door.

Things aren't all staid in Milwaukee, as shown by this rather fanciful take on a Chicago-style bungalow. The round entry tower is a little unusual, but the ceramic ridge tiles are the most fun. Tiles like this would barely show up on a tile roof, but on an asphalt-shingle roof, well, they kind of make the house look like a sea serpent.

ABOVE: This one is right on the edge of not being a bungalow at all, having veered a little too close to Romantic Revival, except for the windows. But how can you not like a house with a teal blue-and-pink roof?

RIGHT: Here's a quintessential Chicago bungalow, from its basement window arc, round-top door, art-glass windows, green-tile roof, limestone trim, and diamond-pattern shingling on the dormer. It even has its window box, unlike most. It's difficult to see, but only the front has the more expensive gold brick, while the sides utilize the darker (and much cheaper) common brick. This was the way of Chicago bungalows.

ON THE STREET

THAT ART WILL MAKE OUR STREETS AS BEAUTIFUL AS THE WOODS, AS
ELEVATING AS THE MOUNTAIN-SIDES: IT WILL BE A PLEASURE AND A REST,
AND NOT A WEIGHT UPON THE SPIRITS TO COME FROM THE OPEN
COUNTRY INTO A TOWN; EVERY MAN'S HOUSE WILL BE FAIR AND DECENT,
SOOTHING TO HIS MIND AND HELPFUL TO HIS WORK: ALL THE WORKS OF
MAN THAT WE LIVE AMONGST AND HANDLE WILL BE IN HARMONY WITH
NATURE, WILL BE REASONABLE AND BEAUTIFUL: YET ALL WILL BE SIMPLE AND
INSPIRITING, NOT CHILDISH NOR ENERVATING; FOR AS NOTHING OF
BEAUTY AND SPLENDOUR THAT MAN'S MIND AND HAND MAY
COMPASS SHALL BE WANTING FROM OUR PUBLIC BUILDINGS, SO IN NO
PRIVATE DWELLING WILL THERE BE ANY SIGNS OF WASTE, POMP, OR
INSOLENCE, AND EVERY MAN WILL HAVE HIS SHARE OF THE BEST.

WILLIAM MORRIS

There are many similarities between our time and the period in which bungalows were being built: rapid technological change, large numbers of immigrants, changes in work patterns and jobs, and differing opinions on what direction to take as Americans in a new century. There are also differences. In the early twentieth century there were

Though shallow, the front porch of a Seattle bungalow has room for a teak bench and a sling chair for relaxing. The far end is enclosed by a glass window to protect the porch from the prevailing winds. Beadboard (narrow tongue-and-groove boards with a V-groove down the center) is a traditional porch ceiling material.

A large lot allows this Memphis bungalow to sprawl in proper bungalow fashion. Its multiple gables are decorated with delicate scroll-sawn designs in the vents, while large knee braces constructed of three two-by-sixes sandwiched together add another attractive element to the facade. The front door is set off by large windows with multi-light transoms on both sides. Rectangular pillars of red brick sit on robust limestone bases. The porte cochere serves as an extension to the porch, with the porch steps sheltered underneath its gable.

A shed roof shelters a deep front porch that runs the full width of the front on a Memphis bungalow. Substantial limestone pillars flanked by equally massive corbels provide more support than the roof actually requires, but give the home a certain presence when viewed from the street. A large front door with sidelights provides a gracious entry. And in spite of all the Arts and Crafts ideals about nature and fitting the home into the landscape, most bungalow builders took the easy way out and installed a path that went straight from the sidewalk to the front door.

few cars, middle-class women for the most part did not work outside the home, and many household needs could be delivered. Unlike most contemporary houses, including those purporting to be "craftsman," presenting a front facade that is mostly garage, most historic bungalows offer their best face to the street, and are oriented toward the front. A generous front porch, its roof often supported on massive columns, welcomes residents and guests. Hard as it may be to believe, people actually used to sit on the front porch in nice weather and talk to their neighbors. On some bungalows the porch may wrap around the side as well, possibly to a pair of French doors opening off the dining room. A three part "Chicago window" is often a feature of the front facade, with an interesting muntin pattern, and perhaps a flower box underneath. Shorter piers on the porch or next to the front steps may support planters or built-in flower boxes—another way of bringing nature into the house. At the sidewalk, there may be an arbor over the path that leads to the house, covered with climbing roses or morning glories. The house itself may be covered with vines or wisteria—some porches had pergolas for just this purpose. Wide eaves shelter the walls, and as Charles Keeler wrote in *The Simple Home*, "The decorative value of shadows cannot well be overestimated . . . A house without eaves always seems to me like a hat without a brim, or like a man who has lost his eyebrows."

ABOVE: The shallow pitch of the porch gable contrasts with the steeper pitch of the main roof on a bungalow in British Columbia. The front facade is straight-forwardly symmetrical, with the stairs in the center leading directly to a one-light front door. A simple railing of square spindles is anchored by slightly tapered columns with simple moldings.

RIGHT: The entrance to this tiny guest cottage in southern California is marked by two humongous stone piers support-ing a bougainvillea-covered pergola. Not only are the piers huge, almost taller than the house itself, the stones they're made out of are seriously big as well.

Those who know me know that I don't think much of new bungalows, not while there are old ones to be saved. But these new bungalows in Memphis's Evergreen Historic District are very well done. Built on a swath of land that had been cleared by the state for a highway (a highway eventually stopped by local citizens), these homes are the product of a fairly rigid set of guidelines set up for new development within the historic district. Possibly the most important of these guidelines was the decree that garages had to be in the back (there are alleys). Traditional local materials: red brick, limestone, stucco, and wood had to be used on the exteriors, and the houses had to be either bungalows or foursquares (there are a couple farther down the street), which are the predominant house forms in the district. Only wooden windows could be used, another important rule. Although I am sure that inside these are all spray-textured drywall and two-story living rooms and MDF, when the landscaping matures they will look little different from the other homes in the neighborhood. I do kind of miss the porte cocheres, though.

THE PLACE BETWEEN

The porch is a place of transition—it is neither inside, nor is it completely outside. It may be a place to pass through or a place to linger. Much was made of the porch at the time, as part of the Arts and Crafts ideal was the blurring of inside and outside space, as well as the belief that life in the open air was healthy and uplifting. In colder climates, porch screens could be exchanged for glass to make a winter sunroom; come summer, the screens could go back in again. Some bungalows had a U-shaped plan that allowed for an open-air patio between the two wings, which provided protection from the wind and more privacy. The need for privacy, though apparently less than ours, was not ignored. Screens of flowering vines, walls of lattice, or roll-up shades were all suggested for porches. Porches were expected to be furnished, with wooden or wicker furniture, Indian rugs or blankets, porch swings, tables, and plants. Some porches were essentially built in the same way as indoor rooms, merely missing a couple of walls.

LEFT: The space between the two wings of an Altadena, California, bungalow provides a sheltered area for lounging or entertaining, anchored by a gigantic stone fireplace with stone benches on either side. Even in the warm climate of southern California, it cools off enough at night for a fire to be welcome. Wouldn't Fred and Wilma have felt right at home here?

OPPOSITE: Originally built as an open porch with a view of the mountains, the porch of this southern California bungalow was later enclosed, and a new open porch added beyond it. Bi-fold windows allow it to be opened up to the outside in warm weather, and rough-cut beams and a tile floor give it a relaxed, informal look. Decorated with Monterey furniture as well as Arts and Crafts pieces, it provides a sheltered spot to relax. Monterey furniture was made by the Mason Manufacturing Company of Los Angeles from 1929 to 1943, in direct response to the popular Spanish revival of the 1920s. Although based on sixteenth- and seventeenth-century Spanish furniture as well as the simple furniture built for the California missions, it has a certain Arts and Crafts influence as well.

Here's a respectably vine-covered porch rendered in two colors of brick, complete with brick corbels providing yet another place to put planters. The piers flanking the steps flair outward for a welcoming look. Why the owners of this Denver bungalow have ignored their concrete planters in favor of the pansy-filled redwood box on the ground is unclear.

LEFT: The once open dining porch of an Eagle Rock, California, bungalow was later enclosed as a sunroom. A wicker settee combines with Oriental antiques, bamboo shades, and potted plants (an important element of any sunroom) to provide a relaxing spot for reading or a cup of tea. French doors connect the sunroom to the adjoining dining room.

RIGHT: An admittedly dormant vine climbs up a trellis on a square porch pillar in Vancouver, B.C. The pillar is hollow, constructed using four one-by-twelve boards around the actual supporting member inside (probably a four-by-four). An interesting swooping railing encloses the end of the porch, and the home is painted in the saturated colors that are traditional in Vancouver.

The brawny sandstone pillars and railing of an Eagle Rock home are bathed in the warm glow of the setting winter sun. The dark-stained beadboard ceiling of the porch provides an elegant counterpoint to the simple concrete floor. A banana plant can just be glimpsed in a pot on the far railing—it *is* southern California, after all.

A formerly open front porch has been glassed-in on this Seattle bungalow, using unevenly divided double-hung windows and a multi-light French door with both sidelights and a transom. Subtle arches above the windows and a decorative band of paneling below tie it all together.

Half sheltered, half open is a typical bungalow porch configuration, although this home has an added shallow gable on the open side. Although no longer technically a bungalow after its second-floor addition, the addition has been made to blend seamlessly with the original house, right down to the matching beam ends, window trim, and pebble-dash stucco in the gable. This is how it should be done, people.

The leaded-glass door of a Santa Monica, California, house opens from the porch directly into the living room, as is the case in many bungalows. A large matching window to the right of the door floods the room with light. Simple flat casings with crown molding and corbels are tied together by a band of picture molding running between them. Another band of wide crown molding adorns the juncture of walls and ceiling. An Arts and Crafts grandfather clock anchors one corner of the room next to a wall sconce, while two leather-upholstered chairs and an amusing cabinet table form a small seating area in front of the window.

ENTERING

It seems to us much more friendly, homelike and comfortable to have one

big living room into which one steps directly from the entrance door, or from

a small vestibule if the climate demands such a protection....

GUSTAV STICKLEY

The informality of bungalows was such that many times the front door opened directly into the living room, though this was also a space-saving device. But others were provided with a small entryway or vestibule. Often this contained a small bench or a built in place for hanging coats.

A generous entry hall complete with window seat awaits visitors inside the front door of a Seattle bungalow. Paneled wainscoating topped by a short spindle railing separates the hall from the stair landing with its thirty-two-paned window (and that's reason enough not to paint your interior woodwork). The living room opens to the right of the entry. A medieval-looking brass five-light chandelier hanging from a sturdy chain hangs over a round oak table accented with an embroidered textile. A soft yellow color on the walls complements the dark fir woodwork.

The entry hall in a bungalow, if there was one, was often divided from the living room only by a colonnade like the one in this Oakland, California, home designed by local architect A. W. Smith in 1909. Tapered (there's that word again) columns on a low plinth "pierced" by fake beams with decoratively cut ends make up this colonnade. On either side of a contemporary stained-glass window, two of the home's original sconces feature cast lion's heads on their brass backplates.

The white-painted board-and-batten paneling of another Seattle entry hall forms the background for a console table by Seattle furniture maker Thomas Stangeland, accentuated by a collection of contemporary art pottery.

One of the many doors of the Greene brothers' Duncan-Irwin House in Pasadena sits under a cantilevered gable with an Oriental-looking hanging lantern. Because the home was a remodel of an existing house, the interior rooms have a quality of not being devoted to a particular purpose, and there is no clear-cut "front door." Nonetheless, beautiful art glass, designed by Charles and executed by Emil Lange, decorates this door and its sidelights.

Sun streaming through the front door of the Pratt House by Charles and Henry Greene streaks the oak floor of the living room, proving that a door opening directly into the living room wasn't just a tract bungalow thing. The two wings of the house are connected by this room, which is really more like a very large reception hall than a typical living room. Corresponding doors on the left side lead to the rear terrace.

HEARTH AND HOME

We want a large room to live in; we want an open fire in it because it looks cheerful and the children like it; we want a kitchen that my wife won't mind working in, and we want the house light and warm and pretty.

A HYPOTHETICAL NEW ENGLAND FARMER TALKING TO HIS BUILDER,
AS QUOTED BY GUSTAV STICKLEY

The living room was the most important room in a bungalow. It was usually the largest room, even in a tiny bungalow, and was most often open to the dining room, the two being separated only by a wide doorway or colonnade, allowing both rooms to borrow visual space from the other, making each seem larger, and allowing a more free flowing space. This was a radical change from nineteenth-century houses, with their formal parlors used only for very special occasions, and their back parlors or sitting rooms, the rooms actually used by the family. As Charles Keeler wrote, "The custom of having a front and back parlor is relegated to the limbo of our grandmothers, and in its stead one large living room suffices for family gatherings and the entertainment of friends." Part of this had to do with Arts and Crafts ideas, but on a more practical level, bungalows weren't all that big and there wasn't room for two parlors. Family life was to be centered here, around the hearth, which assumed an almost religious significance, still embodied in the phrase "hearth and home." Even Frank Lloyd Wright, who had remarkably avant-garde ideas about a lot of things, made the hearth (usually with a huge chimney) the central element of his Prairie houses. This was interesting, given that the majority of bungalows had central heat of some sort, so the fire wasn't really being used for warmth. It was more that it satisfied some primal need going back to the discovery of fire by our primitive ancestors, a need which causes us even today to include fireplaces in our homes and make them the focal point of the living room.

A tall colonnade with bookcases separates the living room from the dining room of a Seattle bungalow. The bookcases, with simple leaded-glass doors, are a continuation of the ones that flank the living room's clinker brick fireplace. A shallow niche in the bricks provides display space for small pots. Light fixtures hang from metal wall brackets above the fireplace. A sponged wall treatment in shades of yellow harmonizes with the dark stained woodwork.

Woodwork left in a natural finish was also a defining feature of the bungalow. Woodwork was second only to the fireplace in its quasi-religious significance, and that it would be done that way was almost taken for granted. It was, after all, made up entirely of old-growth timber.

ABOVE: In some bungalows, the living room and dining room weren't divided at all. In this Berkeley home, a tile-fronted fireplace provides a visual division between the dining room in the foreground and the living room. Bungalow fireplaces almost universally had high windows on either side, like the ones shown here. Built-in cupboards in the living room provide storage. The side chair next to the sideboard matches the settle (believed to be from somewhere in Scandinavia) in the living room. The light fixtures in both rooms were made by metalsmith Audel Davis.

LEFT: A simple squared arch was a common device for separating rooms, as shown in this Berkeley home. Sliding pocket doors or French doors were also common solutions. This allowed one room to borrow visual space from another, important with the limited square footage of some bungalows. Bungalow dwellers had less furniture than is common today, and were less likely to have sofas (or even settles) than we are. The norm was a lot of individual chairs, like the Morris chair in the corner and the rocker in the foreground, accompanied by a small octagonal taboret or other small side table. A library table was also found in many bungalow living rooms, because in the days before television, people used to read, hard as that may be to believe. Coffee tables as we know them were unheard of.

In the living room of a Chicago bungalow, it's obvious how the front bay floods the room with light through numerous windows. By the 1920s, when most Chicago bungalows were built, there was somewhat less emphasis on huge amounts of interior woodwork and paneling, although whatever woodwork was installed was still generally not painted. Much of it was painted at a later date, as this was. In spite of that, this room clearly shows the many ways in which the severe lines of Arts and Crafts furniture were meant to be softened by curtains, pillows, rugs, table scarves, and so forth. The settle in front of the window, as well as the leather-cushioned rocker on the right, are decorated with hand-embroidered linen pillows, while the screen in the corner is draped with embroidered table scarves (not the usual use for these but a good way to show off a collection). A round leather-top table is home to a plant in a hand-decorated pot, and a large collection of other art pottery is scattered around the room. But the best thing in this room is the tiny, child-size Morris chair, in reality, a salesman's sample.

An Arts and Crafts living room was added to this 1901 Colonial revival home in Tacoma, Washington, in 1907. The home, built for department store magnate Henry Rhodes, was designed by Tacoma architects Russell and Babcock. The addition was designed by Frederick Heath, another Tacoma architect. The large fireplace and hearth is faced with green Grueby tile with an inset of sailing ships and waves. Above the fireplace, the Latin motto translates as "I too am in Arcadia", while the hand-painted mural (new) in the frieze illustrate the views that would have been seen in each direction if there were no other houses in the way. The battens below the windows are interspersed with sections of plaster rather than the usual boards. A library table in front of the windows holds a hammered-copper lamp with a mica shade centered on an embroidered table round. Next to the rocker, a Tiffany dragonfly floor lamp sits next to a peacock vase filled with, you guessed it, peacock feathers. The sunflowers in the foreground are another nod to the Aesthetic Movement. And check out the massive pieces of Douglas fir that make up the two vertical sides of the fireplace—those are some big pieces of wood. The fir ceiling beams are also structural. All the wood in this room had to be stripped of paint.

The living room of the Duncan-Irwin House in Pasadena features a large tiled fireplace with a raised hearth, perfect for extra seating. On the left, a window seat provides a perfect place for viewing the scenic beauty of the arroyo. A flat casing that serves for window and door lintels as well as picture molding encircles the room. Doweled finger joints join its outside corners. Above, an elaborate light fixture (of a type known as a "shower," with several lights hanging from chains or pipes, though this one is more like a deluge) illuminates a slatted oak settle and a Roycroft library table, while two Morris chairs on either side of the fireplace offer a relaxing place for conversation or just staring into the fire.

ABOVE: New tile with pinecone accents has been applied to the fireplace in the living room of a 1911 Milwaukee home. The mantel and fireplace surround are stained birch. To the right, an armoire holds the various modern technology we now expect to have in our living room. Two new art-glass sconces with "hipped roofs" flank a gold-leafed print of irises. The floors in this room are maple. At the ceiling, an angular crown molding traces the edges of the room.

RIGHT: The 1906 Bolton House, also by Greene and Greene, has had its Grueby tile and brass inlaid fireplace restored after an unfortunate 1950s modernization in which the fireplaces were ripped out and all the mahogany and Port Orford cedar woodwork was painted white. As in many of their houses, the top casings continue as picture molding, tying the door and window openings together. Flat moldings, not really beams in this case, form a decorative design on the ceiling that is integrated with the base for the hanging art-glass light fixture. The built-in bench to the left shows the cloud-lift motif of which the Greenes were so fond. The wheat color of the walls and the taupe shade of the frieze brings out the red tones of the woodwork. The Arts and Crafts coffee table is, of course, contemporary.

The purplish hues of clinker bricks complement the dark fir woodwork in this Berkeley brownshingle (the local term for shingled Arts and Crafts homes). High windows on either side of the chimney, a very typical feature in bungalows, allow for bookcases or other built-ins below. In this case, there is only one bookcase on the left, the right side being paneled to allow for opening the French doors that lead to a sunken den at the right. Native American baskets decorate the mantel, while a Navajo rug anchors the Limbert rocker and Morris chair. On the round table, hammered copper pots keep company with a small painting by Gottardo Piazzoni.

There's just no end to the fun you can have with clinker bricks. On this Berkeley fireplace, in a home by Leola Hall, who was unusual for her time in being not only a designer of homes but also a builder, clinker brick corbels hold up a clinker brick mantel in a fir-paneled living room. The drawback of a clinker brick mantel? Not very many level places to display your art pottery, and difficult to dust.

Clinker bricks are mixed with other bricks and some eccentric brickwork (yeah, that's the technical term) to make an interesting fireplace for a Memphis bungalow. A corbeled shelf on the chimney holds candles, while above the firebox, bricks form the letter "A", the initial of the first owners.

Diagonal squares of gold spotted brick stand out from the face of a small fireplace flanked by the usual glass-doored bookcases. Because this Milwaukee bungalow has a gas fireplace (you can just make out the logs behind the copper fire screen), it doesn't require a chimney, which allows the trio of stained-glass windows above the mantel. The birch woodwork is stained a deep reddish hue, which makes a nice contrast with the pale blue-green of the walls. Twenties-style candle sconces bracket the windows. This small room is one of those extra rooms that has no set purpose, commonly found off the living room or the entry hall in many bungalows.

Many Chicago bungalows had only the suggestion of a fireplace, as this one does. I wonder if people put in those fake fireplace things with the red light bulb and the spinning cylinder of tinfoil? There *is* an electrical outlet for it. Anyway, this one has the requisite bookcases made a little more interesting by their asymmetry. Glass shelves have replaced the original wood shelves. No doubt the brick was not painted when the house was first built. A cushy Morris chair and an art-glass lamp complement a fine collection of art pottery and other Arts and Crafts objects displayed on the "fireplace."

LEFT: Inside a Prairie-style Memphis bungalow (see an exterior photo on pg. 11, an arched stone fireplace is surmounted by a mirror which reflects the elaborate red gum-wood box beams and arches of the living room. Though it is a little difficult to see in the photo, the woodwork is joined with dovetails and pegs, especially obvious in the uprights above the fireplace. A band of casements runs along two sides of the room, the high sills making it easier to arrange furniture.

ABOVE: Though quite unprepossessing from outside (see pg. 107), this large 1910 bungalow built for Eagle Rock minister Alfred Walden Hare has a large 27-by-16-foot living room that Reverend Walden and his wife Grace used for entertaining parishioners. A tiled fireplace with a thick mantel supported by square corbels is accompanied by bookcases with leaded-glass doors. The bookcases are shorter than usual, which allows the casement windows above to be larger, flooding the room with light. The most unusual feature of the room is the complex box-beam ceiling, which still retains its original beam lights. Bare lightbulbs were the norm. More square corbels hold up a plate rail–like crown molding above the windows and doors.

LEFT: The woodwork in Memphis bungalows is invariably red gumwood, also known as tupelo (even though tupelo is black gum and belongs to a different species entirely). This woodwork, once painted Pepto-Bismol pink, was refinished by a previous owner to a reddish color. The limestone fireplace has a Rookwood tile hearth, and is home to a set of 1930s-era gas logs that don't really have flames; instead, pinholes allow the burning gas to wreathe the logs in a sort of ghostly blue emanation. Above the battened wainscoting, the present owner has stenciled a landscape frieze. Beam lights with mica shades hang from chains, complementing the contemporary mica lamp on the table below.

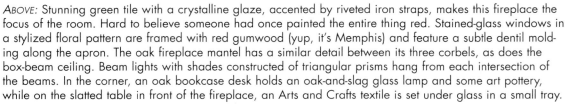

ABOVE: Stunning green tile with a crystalline glaze, accented by riveted iron straps, makes this fireplace the focus of the room. Hard to believe someone had once painted the entire thing red. Stained-glass windows in a stylized floral pattern are framed with red gumwood (yup, it's Memphis) and feature a subtle dentil molding along the apron. The oak fireplace mantel has a similar detail between its three corbels, as does the box-beam ceiling. Beam lights with shades constructed of triangular prisms hang from each intersection of the beams. In the corner, an oak bookcase desk holds an oak-and-slag glass lamp and some art pottery, while on the slatted table in front of the fireplace, an Arts and Crafts textile is set under glass in a small tray.

RIGHT: A large Batchelder-tile fireplace with landscape-tile insets anchors one end of a very large living room that stretches across the entire front of a U-shaped Altadena, California, bungalow (the home, at 3,600 square feet, *is* kind of pushing the bungalow envelope, in spite of its one-story height. See page 159 for a photo of this home's outdoor fireplace). The home, designed in 1915 by Edgar H. Dorr, a young Los Angeles architect, was built for William E. Ruth and his wife. Mr. Ruth was in the liquor business, so perhaps they entertained a lot, and the business must have been lucrative enough (at least until Prohibition in 1919) that they could afford the high-quality finishes that characterize the home. An L-shaped bench provides seating on one side of the fireplace, while on the other side, a bookcase with a distinctive muntin pattern in its glass doors mirrors two identical bookcases that flank a window seat at the other end of the room. Stained-glass windows in a more traditional pattern than is usually found in bungalows frame the fireplace. All of the woodwork is mahogany. An unfortunate coat of "popcorn" spray texture on the ceiling will eventually be removed.

RIGHT: A tall fireplace faced with mottled tile has an angled overmantel of bookmatched red gumwood veneer. Two corbels made from three pieces of wood sandwiched together, as well as a wide crown molding, support the mantel. The olive color on the walls and between the battens picks up the same tones in the tile. French doors with beveled glass lead into a study beyond.

Batchelder tile wraps around the sides of the living room fireplace of the Gould House in Ventura, designed by Henry Greene. The tall landscape tiles on the sides are giant sequoias, one of Mrs. Gould's favorite trees, while the smaller tiles feature birds. The Goulds had commissioned the home from the Greenes in shortly before World War I, but the project kept being put on hold for various reasons. By the time design began in earnest in 1923, Charles Greene had moved to Carmel, leaving the project to Henry. The living room fireplace backs up to another in the sunroom behind, sharing the same chimney. The living room has been repainted in an approximation of the original colors. The woodwork is Port Orford cedar, with a slight greenish cast to the stain.

ABOVE: A slightly rosy cast in the color of the wire-cut "reptile" bricks that make up the fireplace sparked the color scheme for a bungalow living room in Milwaukee. A large collection of Niloak Mission Swirl pottery lines the dark oak mantel, lit by two Art Deco sconces above. The tray ceiling is wallpapered and a bowl chandelier with a hand-painted porcelain shade hangs from the center. A hand-painted fire screen showing a sunset enhances the hearth. A window seat with fabric covered cushions also disguises the radiators.

LEFT: A slightly pointed arch distinguishes the firebox of this tile fireplace. Three carved corbels support the mantel. The buttery color of the walls works well with the wood trim and also picks up the colors in the print above the fireplace.

But it was also part of the blurring of inside and out so prized by the Arts and Crafts Movement designers. (There were a few people who actually worried about the depletion of old-growth forests, even then, but for the most part they were ignored.) Stickley wrote, "We need not dwell upon the importance of using a generous amount of woodwork to give an effect of permanence, homelikeness, and rich warm color in a room. Anyone who has ever entered a house in which the friendly natural wood is used in the form of wainscoting, beams, and structural features of all kinds, has only to contrast the impression given by such an interior with that which we receive when we go into the average house…" Often the beams and structural features were fake, but, as Keeler pointed out, "…they are a most effective decoration with their parallel lines and shadows."

The simplicity of the interior was meant to be enriched and softened with paintings, pottery, embroidery, metalwork, rugs, curtains, and other works of art and craft. People were encouraged to take up crafts of their own, echoing William Morris's belief that all people had a spark of creativity.

That books were important is evidenced by the fact that almost no bungalow was without built-in bookcases. After all, before television, people actually used to read books.

The other end of the Altadena living room shown on page 183 has two more built-in bookcases on either side of a window seat that looks out into the exotic plantings of the garden. Stained-glass casement windows with a design completely different from those at the other end of the room open inward to let in breezes. A library table, a Morris chair with an ottoman, and an upholstered rocker make this a pleasant place for reading or conversation.

RIGHT: An inviting inglenook with a simple brick fireplace is set off into one corner of the large living room of a Seattle bungalow, and separated by a colonnade from the rest of the room. Padded benches with a plethora of pillows offer a comfortable spot for sitting by the fire in the evening or on a rainy Seattle afternoon.

OPPOSITE: From the exterior, the new two-story living room of this Seattle bungalow merely looks like a large dormer added to the side-gabled home. Inside, the soaring ceiling is crowned with criss-crossing fir box beams with art-glass pendant lighting. A line of molding and a Bradbury and Bradbury wallpaper border at the original ceiling line help keep the room from having the "upended coffin" feel that rooms with high ceilings can sometimes have. Reproduction Arts and Crafts furniture surrounds a newly tiled fireplace with a gas insert. Lighting has been added to the bookcases on either side. A colonnade with square columns separates the living room from the dining room, which has a conventional ceiling height.

ABOVE: A cozy fir-paneled nook next to a clinker brick fireplace is lit by sunlight filtered through two art-glass windows in a Berkeley home by architect/builder Leola Hall. The deep recess of the smaller window was a Hall hallmark, as it were. Wide panels like these were generally plywood or veneer, rather than full boards. The slatted oak bench is complemented by an oak floor lamp with a stenciled mica shade.

A vintage embroidered pillow and table scarf bring the colors of nature to a cozy nook with oak furniture and a mica-shaded copper lamp at the Riordan House in Flagstaff.

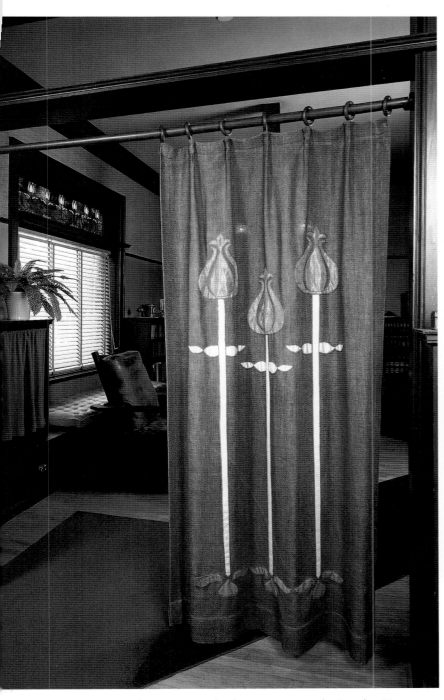

Speckled brick forms a simple fireplace in this Pasadena home. Small mica-shaded round lanterns hang from chains below the mantel. Pleated linen drapes hang from square wooden rods, and the putty color of the walls provides a neutral background for paintings and art pottery. My stand on recessed lighting is well known: don't.

Original portieres (door curtains) divide two rooms at the Riordan House. Appliquéd and embroidered with tulips, the design echoes the tulips in the art-glass window transoms of the house. Few of these textiles have survived.

FEAST FOR THE SENSES

Difficult as it may be to believe, in bungalows, people ate in the dining room. Eating dinner together was considered to be an important part of family life, when news of the day would be exchanged. Not like today, when the dining room is lucky to be used on holidays and for the occasional dinner party. The dining room in a bungalow was actually meant to be used, not just for dinner, but even for other meals. Although with the advent of breakfast nooks, sometimes breakfast, lunch, or tea would take place more informally in the kitchen, but dinner was always eaten in the dining room. Because it was often open to the living room, it shared similar decor—lots of woodwork, often a wainscoting topped with a plate rail (perfect for showing off your decorative objects), and almost always a built-in china cabinet or sideboard. Some bungalows had French doors leading to an outdoor porch for summertime meals in the open air. It is theoretically possible, even now, to eat in the dining room.

Some bungalows, even quite modest ones, may have had a butler's pantry between the dining room and the kitchen. This is where dishes, glassware, and silverware were kept, often table linens as well, and it frequently included a sink for washing the dishes, as it was believed to be unsanitary to have dishwashing and food preparation in the same room.

PRIVATE MOMENTS

In many bungalows, there would be a small room off to one side that was either set up as a study or den (always for the man of the house), or else with its function not so obviously defined. A study usually contained more built-in bookcases, possibly a built-in desk, and other built-in cabinets.

Usually there was lots of woodwork here as well, and other things that would be considered masculine. This is where the man of the house might retire after dinner to read the paper, smoke a cigar, or pay the bills. If the function was less defined, it might just be a small extra room that could be used as a guest room, a nursery, a sewing room, a music room, a library, or whatever the members of the household desired. It might contain a Murphy bed for guests, another space-saving idea.

An eleven-light-shower fixture with more chains than Marley's ghost hangs from a series of interlocking decorative boards on the ceiling of Greene and Greene's Duncan-Irwin House in Pasadena. A series of horizontal boards encircles the room—a crown molding, a picture rail (a pegged scarf joint in this molding can be glimpsed just above the hammered-copper lamp on the sideboard), and a plate rail, as well as the baseboard. Above the tiled fireplace, a composition of horizontal and vertical boards frames a hanging plein air painting. Simple casement windows with a doubled horizontal muntin bar are softened by linen scrim curtains hung on square wooden rods, while above, transoms of amber-colored art glass filter the light. A glimpse of the butler's pantry can be seen through the open door next to a wooden wall sconce. There is more antique Arts and Crafts furniture in this room than you can shake a stick at.

The dining room of this particular Chicago bungalow also encompasses the staircase. A layered-glass and wrought-iron fixture is suspended over a round Limbert dining table, surrounded by L. & J.G. Stickley chairs (Gus had many brothers). On the table, a matte-green vase is centered on a runner embroidered with stylized flowers. The L. & J. G. Stickley sideboard holds a Tiffany lamp and more art pottery below a row of framed French advertising posters that were produced between 1895 and 1900. A Gustav Stickley buffet by the stairs hold matte-green pottery and an Art Nouveau lamp.

The vogue for built-ins had a few critics, as shown in this poem published in *The Architect and Engineer* in 1914:

This is the song of the bungalow,

With a buffet built in the wall

And a disappearing bed beneath

That won't disappear at all;

A song of the folding Morris chair

That never will fold until

You plant your weary carcass there

And sprawl in a sudden spill;

The song of the dinky writing desk

That hangs from a sliding door

Which sends you kiting galley west

Until you write no more;

The song of the pretty porcelain tub

With a flour bin below,

And a leak that springs on the bread-to-be

While on the floor runs liquid dough;

A song of the handy kitchenette

That is almost two feet square

And all undefiled by the sordid job

Of cooking dinner there;

A song of the lidded window seat

Where no one could ever sit,

And of plate racks that come crashing down,

And of shelves no books would fit;

A song of pantry and bureau drawers

That will never go in or out—

Oh, a song for all "built-in features"

That we read so much about.

Kind friend, if you capture a bungalow,

Keep it, and your soul, unmarred,

By taking a kit and a sleeping bag

And living right out in the yard.

Crossed table runners were the thing in bungalows, rather than table-cloths or place mats. These are stenciled with pinecone designs, a popular motif, and set with the owner's collection of turquoise Fiesta Ware. Admittedly, Fiesta Ware wasn't introduced until 1936, but it *was* designed by Frederick Rhead, a potter who had worked for many Arts and Crafts potteries, including Weller, Roseville, Arequipa, and the American Encaustic Tiling Company. A hand-painted bowl fixture complements the beam lights that hang from junctures in the gumwood box beams of the ceiling. The frieze is highlighted with a stencil design of trees, bringing a touch of nature into the home. Grooves in the edges of the battens add a subtle detail to the usual bungalow paneling.

Other built-ins included linen closets, telephone nooks, ironing boards, desks, benches, clothes chutes, window seats, milk or icing doors (for the icebox), liquor cabinets, etc.

ABOVE: Miniature versions of the tapered columns supporting the porch roof outside are found on many dining rooms' built-in sideboards. This particular one is unusual in that it has an open shelf above its leaded-glass doors. The trim around it, which matches the other door and window trim in the home, has a continuation of the side casings above the top casing, and the top casings rise to a shallow peak in the center. A sponged finish on the walls sets off the woodwork and the square-canopied sconce, which matches the four lights of the shower fixture that hang from square linked chains.

LEFT: The frieze area above the paneling and plate rail in this Portland, Oregon, dining room has been hand painted by the owner with a mural loosely based on William Morris tapestries. The figures in the original tapestries were drawn by Edward Burne-Jones. This kind of do-it-yourself artwork was exactly the sort of things that the Arts and Crafts Movement encouraged. Below the plate rail, an antique Chinese icebox provides storage and display space. The Arts and Crafts–style table and chairs are new.

Windows were often incorporated into dining room sideboards, as well as art glass. This one has both. Green slag glass enhances the lower doors, which hang from interesting corner hinges, while hints of green glass combine with caramel and purple glass in the upper doors. The two upper cabinets are somewhat unusual in having leaded glass on their sides as well. Both of the upper cabinets have thru-tenons going every which way, possibly the designer having gone just a tad overboard on the whole "expressed structure" thing. Under the window, a shelf with elaborate corbels and cutouts provides display space for one of the owners' collection of monkeys (there are more on the high plate rail above). The whole sideboard has a greyish stain over the Douglas fir, which was a popular treatment. As elaborate as this cabinet is, it's in a fairly modest bungalow.

LEFT: The design of an oak built-in sideboard in a Memphis home just goes to show that Arts and Crafts was open to all kinds of interpretation. Besides its classical dentil molding (which is matched by similar molding at the ceiling line), this cabinet features linen-fold carving on the doors, fluted vertical moldings at the sides, and beaded edges on the inset drawers, and lozenge-shaped leaded glass on the central doors. Yet the stylized floral design of the art-glass window above, the simple window and door trim, and the design of the chandelier are well within Arts and Crafts parameters. The wall battens are separate by a textured wall covering made to resemble leather. Custom window coverings inspired by the design of the stained-glass window were hand-woven by textile artist Eleanor Lux of Eureka Springs, Arkansas. The copper bowl on the table's embroidered scarf has a repoussé design of various fruits, and the Stickley reproduction chairs have inlaid designs that also echo the design of the art-glass window.

OPPOSITE: Redwood ceiling beams and paneling were utilized by architect Julia Morgan in the dining room of a Berkeley bungalow. An uncommon leaded-glass design made up of a series of rounds decorates the doors of the upper cabinet, while the lower doors have subtle V grooves where the edges of the three boards that make up the center panels meet. The same detail is used in the upright paneling made from one-by-eight boards. Above the plate rail, the frieze is covered with original gilded linen. The chandelier was made by Seattle craftsman Larry Willits. The generic round table is surrounded by Limbert chairs with leather seats.

ABOVE: The butler's pantry in a Berkeley home still has its original cabinets, hardware, and wooden counters, though someone chose to paint it all pink in the 1950s. The tall cabinet on the left is a cooler cabinet (vented to the outside and used as an adjunct to the icebox). Just below it on the left are two tilt-out bins for large bags of flour and sugar, though in our time, mostly used for pet food and recycling storage. The bin handles and cupboard catches were the most common kind of cabinet hardware, not only in butler's pantries but also in kitchens.

RIGHT: The dining room of a 1901 home in Tacoma, Washington, has a more transitional feel than the newer (1907) living room beyond. Above the board-and-batten paneling on the lower walls, shallow cabinets with leaded-glass doors set atop the plate rail are used for displaying stemware. A combination gas and electric chandelier hangs over an oval oak table and chairs, set on a reproduction Arts and Crafts rug. An oak plant stand holds a large piece of Van Briggle pottery filled with curly willow branches in front of the lace and velvet window curtains. New wallpaper from Bradbury and Bradbury covers the ceiling and frieze.

A new Greene and Greene–style chandelier with a much simplified art-glass pattern was designed by Randell Makinson and constructed by Douglas Hawkins and Jane Heald to replace the missing original in the dining room of the Gould House in Ventura, California. It is centered over an oak table. The home, designed by Henry Greene in the 1920s, is understated compared to the brothers' "ultimate bungalows" such as the Blacker and Gamble Houses in Pasadena. Nonetheless, it has an unpretentious charm that befits its original use as a small home in the country. The built-in is recessed between two sets of casement windows with doubled horizontal muntin bars. (Note that the upper bar is subtly thinner than the one below.) Over the built-in, more casement windows with sidelights are glazed with art glass in a design of birds, butterflies, and flowers. The drawer pulls and trim were carved by Henry Greene on-site. The pegged wooden curtain rods are original to the house.

The rough-sawn redwood paneling and beams evoke a barn-like ambience appropriate to the country location of this 1909 southern California bungalow. A greyish stain gives the appearance of weathering and contrasts with the door and window casings. The beams have been distressed to give a hand-hewn look, and then stenciled with Native American designs. Navajo rugs on the fir floors continue the theme. A long oval Stickley Brothers table is accompanied by ladder-back chairs of unknown provenance and set with Bauer dinnerware from the 1930s. An L & J.G. Stickley glass-door china cabinet near the French doors holds more dinnerware. The wrought-iron chandelier probably dates to the 1920s. The painted hutch was commissioned for the house. A Roseville jardiniere in the Mostique pattern stands on a pedestal under a hand-tinted photo of Yosemite National Park.

Art-glass casements surround three sides of the dining room in a Milwaukee bungalow. The ones on the left open to a music room that is just off the entry. The geometric design of the art glass shows the pervasive influence of the Prairie School in the Midwest. The built-in oak sideboard extends the full length of the room and its glass doors mirror the design of the windows, while beveled mirrors set into the center section reflect whatever is displayed there. The plaster ceiling is coved above the windows and then recessed, the recess being set off by a plaster molding of grapes and vines. A bowl chandelier hangs from rods over a traditionally styled table.

Square pillars support the petite upper cabinets of this sideboard while more leaded-glass doors combine with drawers below. Square corbel blocks support a flat overhanging molding at the top of the cabinet, and are echoed by other corbel blocks under the plate rail and above the door (back left corner) that leads to the kitchen. Stained Douglas fir paneling contrasts with the reddish wood of the contemporary mahogany Arts and Crafts table and chairs. A faux Roseville rabbit vase filled with flowers is flanked by real Roseville candlesticks. The dining room is small compared to the large living room of this home—apparently Reverend Hare, the original owner, didn't entertain parishioners over dinner.

A colonnade with new hanging mica lanterns (as well as the matching chandelier) by Seattle craftsman Michael Ashford divides the living and dining rooms of a 1906 Seattle bungalow. The fairly simple design of this dining room has no paneling, only a plate rail and picture molding above. A small built-in corner cabinet with glass doors provides storage, while an oak server against the back wall features doors with panels held together by wedge-shaped "butterfly keys." A five-panel swinging door on the right leads to the kitchen. This room also illustrates how dark woodwork really needs a saturated color on the walls for balance, for less contrast and a more harmonious whole.

A mottled-tile fireplace with a corbeled mantel is an added feature in the dining room of a Berkeley home. Many bungalows had fireplaces in other rooms as well as the living room. The fireplace is flanked by cabinets whose glass doors have a pattern similar to the window muntins of the home, while the built-in sideboard has leaded glass in its doors. Above the paneling and plate rail, the frieze is painted in a soft mottled green, which sets off the gold frames of the plein air paintings. A coffered ceiling retains the original beam lights. The table and chairs are by Gustav Stickley.

The oak sideboard extends nearly the entire length of the dining room and is centered on three Prairie-style art-glass windows in a Milwaukee home. Wood muntins combine with leaded glass in the doors of the side cabinets, which also have leaded-glass panels on the sides. The dropped ceiling over the sideboard curves down to meet the tops of the tall cabinets, which are on the same level as the plate rail. Plum-colored walls have been stenciled by the owner with an elaborate design. The maple floors feature a decorative inset in the doorway. A shelf built over the radiator provides a window seat in the entry hall on the left, and a pair of French doors separates the entry from the front door, providing an "air lock" in cold weather.

Angled cabinets at the top make for a "bay window" effect on the sideboard of an English-influenced Arts and Crafts home in Milwaukee. Beveled mirrors reflect the owners' collection of silver, while more glass doors below allow for further display of serving pieces. Above the built-in, pairs of corbels hold a narrow secondary plate rail (the other plate rail is even with the bottom of the upper cabinet). In the corner, a glimpse of one of the original floral-design light fixtures can be seen hanging from the center of one of the panels of the coffered ceiling. Wallpaper in a medallion design picks up the colors of the oak woodwork.

The restored dining room of Greene and Greene's Bolton house had its walls redone with board-and-batten mahogany paneling that matches the paneling in the entry hall. Pegged scarf joints join the boards of the picture rail, while above it the soft gold color of the textured sand plaster provides a counterpoint to the reddish tones of the wood. An art-glass ceiling fixture and wall-mounted sconces were features repeated in various forms in many Greene-designed homes.

ABOVE: The butler's pantry in Greene and Greene's 1909 Spinks House in Pasadena features simple detailing in Douglas fir. Joints pegged with dowels secure the corners of the cabinet frames, into which are set sliding glass doors. (The lower doors under the nickel-silver sink with its gooseneck faucet have been replaced.) The sculpted handles of the two drawers on the left are another of the subtle details for which the brothers were known.

ABOVE: This sideboard is topped by art-glass windows in a shamrock pattern, and the same pattern is repeated in the leaded-glass doors. Barely seen at the far end of the sideboard are some interesting triangular corbels. The tray ceiling above is edged with decorative plaster moldings, including a rather classical egg-and-dart molding just above the Schumacher wallpaper border. The woodwork in this room is walnut, pretty high dollar for a bungalow. On the back wall, a painting by illustrator Charles Livingston Bull is displayed above a large 1902 Avon Faience pot by Frederick Hurton Rhead that rests on an antique Chinese table. The generic table and chairs have an English Arts and Crafts look, especially in the carving on the chair backs. On the table, a Weller cattail bowl with a kingfisher flower frog is centered on a round table scarf embroidered with dragons. The original chandelier is silverplate over brass and shows an Art Nouveau influence. The camel sculpture is an antique from Czechoslovakia, and was chosen (obviously) to go with the painting.

A simple and extremely typical built-in rendered in Douglas fir anchors one end of the dining room in a Berkeley home. Miniature tapered pillars appear to support the top cabinet with its leaded-glass doors in a stock pattern. In the center, a mirrored pass-through opens to the kitchen. All kinds of prefabricated items could be purchased for bungalows through millwork catalogs—not only sideboards and china cabinets but also colonnades, desks, staircases, fireplace surrounds, mantels, doors, windows, breakfast nooks, kitchen cupboards, etc.

Beyond the (back of) an original appliquéd curtain, a small part of the dining room of the Riordan House in Flagstaff can just be glimpsed. The room is oval and lined with arches. The curved sideboard is set into one of the arched recesses. The dining table and chairs were made especially for the house, and its pointed oval shape was designed to encourage conversation. Curved window seats form part of the oval at one end of the room (at left). Art-glass sconces hang from wooden corbels "chained" to the walls. The blue-green–and–wheat color scheme of the walls is separated by a simple wooden molding.

Hexagonal tiles with an intricate border design comprise the floor of the breakfast room at the Lanterman House in La Cañada-Flintridge, California. French doors open the room to the shaded terrace outside, while a suite of wicker furniture gives a porch-like feel to the space.

Just off the master bedroom of a Berkeley home, a redwood-paneled room of indeterminate usage has been turned into an office. Well, not really an office, actually more of a shrine. The desk is a generic Arts and Crafts piece. Everything in and on the desk (mostly dating to the 1940s), as well as the desk itself, belonged to the owner's mother, who was a newspaper reporter, photographer, and artist. (A photo of her, dressed in an Indian feather headdress, sits in the typewriter.)

LEFT: The generous entry hall of this 1922 Milwaukee bungalow has been turned into a music room. Looking from the front door towards the dining room, on the left a wall of Prairie-influenced art-glass windows are balanced on the right by French doors with a similar pattern, which lead to the living room. More windows between the dining room and the music room increase the sense of openness in the home. The oak woodwork contrasts with the lighter color of the maple floors. The coved ceilings of this room are repeated in the other rooms of the house.

OPPOSITE: The den of a 1912 bungalow in Memphis features a coffered, beamed ceiling, grooved battens, and plain window trim decorated with wooden pyramids at the ends of the top casings. All the woodwork is red gumwood. It has an interesting red stain because the former owner of the home worked for Formby's (maker of wood-finishing products) and used the home for product testing. The original hand-painted bowl fixture hangs from the ceiling. The faint greenish tint of the yellow wall color enhances the woodwork, and stenciling by the owner highlights the frieze. The room is furnished with two Morris chairs upholstered in green leather, and an oak-and-mica lamp on the round oak side table provides light for reading.

ABOVE: In a new bungalow like this one in Lafayette, California, it's possible to build an office that accommodates various twenty-first-century demands while still having an Arts and Crafts look. A box-beamed ceiling complements tall paneling of alternating wide and narrow boards with battens, topped by a high plate rail supported by decorative square-pegged corbels. The room's built-in cabinetry includes lateral files (on the left) and other enclosed storage, and a plethora of bookshelves that allow the owner to display a collection of antique toy cars, trucks, and other methods of transportation.

OPPOSITE: Sitting rooms were another use of extra rooms, usually in larger Arts and Crafts homes. This room has been fitted out with an oak settle, a Monterey chair with ottoman, and a wrought-iron bridge lamp with a mica shade. A small table with a wrought-iron base provides a place to put one's book or cup of tea, while woven-reed shades on the windows filter the light to reduce glare. An Arts and Crafts rug on the fir floor brings together the various colors in the room. The greenish-gold wall color was a popular Arts and Crafts shade.

Architect Julia Morgan added guest quarters to the rear of the 1905 Wadsworth House in Berkeley a few years after the house was built. The living room of the guest house has the same redwood cathedral ceiling as the living room in the main house (see frontispiece), but the walls have been covered with plaster rather than paneling. High windows are used on the back wall due to the slope of the hill. A small clinker-brick fireplace fits neatly between the windows. French doors lead to a diminutive porch on one side. In the foreground, a Stickley Brothers Morris chair and rocker are paired with a generic table. A lamp showing some Prairie School influence has an art-glass shade comprised of two layers of glass. Over the mantel, a painting of Mount Rainier hangs above and Arts and Crafts clock. A reproduction Stickley three-door bookcase just fits under the high windows. Next to it is a Prairie-style armchair by the Boston Chair Company under an oak mirror (probably meant to go in an entry hall, given the coat hooks).

Boy, those Kelmscott settles really get around, don't they? Here's one ensconced in an addition to a Berkeley home, basically built as a family room. Redwood board-and-batten paneling covers the walls, and the leaded-glass windows have been made to match others in the house (see pg. 51). Two pillows covered with Liberty of London "Ianthe" fabric (originally designed as an Art Nouveau wallpaper border in 1902) cushion the settle. An art-glass sconce made by Berkeley craftsman Audel Davis hangs between two contemporary plein air paintings in gold frames. A hand-hammered copper lamp, as well as the candlesticks, bowls, and vase on the mantel, were also made by Davis. An antique kilim covers the floor.

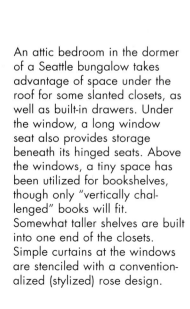

An attic bedroom in the dormer of a Seattle bungalow takes advantage of space under the roof for some slanted closets, as well as built-in drawers. Under the window, a long window seat also provides storage beneath its hinged seats. Above the windows, a tiny space has been utilized for bookshelves, though only "vertically challenged" books will fit. Somewhat taller shelves are built into one end of the closets. Simple curtains at the windows are stenciled with a conventionalized (stylized) rose design.

A very grand Arts and Crafts house like Artemisia in Hollywood, would have walk-in closets (not usually a feature of tiny bungalows). This closet, off the master bedroom, also has a dressing table built in to a recess with an arched top. The fairly simple muntin pattern of the casement windows is surrounded by rather more elaborate oak molding on the inside. And even in the warm climate of southern California, it would still be a luxury to have a radiator in your dressing room for those rare days when it might be a little chilly.

DOMESTIC SCIENCE

Bungalow kitchens were the first "modern" kitchens—they contained the things we still have in kitchens in the twenty-first-century: a sink, a stove, a refrigerator, cabinets, and workspaces. The kitchen was the most complex room in a bungalow, as it is the most complex room in a modern house. But in bungalows it was a workroom, a utilitarian space, rather than the central place in the home it has become in our century. Nonetheless, it was pretty functional even twenty-first century standards and compared to what had come before. Stickley wrote: "… we have paid particular attention to the convenient arrangement of the kitchen…we believe in having the kitchen small, so that extra steps may be avoided, and fitted with every kind of convenience and comfort; with plenty of shelves and cupboards, open plumbing, the hooded range which carries off all odors of cooking, the refrigerator which can be filled from the outside—in fact, everything that tends to save time, strength, and worry…the luxuries of the properly arranged modern kitchen would have been almost unbelievable a generation ago." Whether the kitchen in any given bungalow lived up to those standards depended much on the designer. Since most of the designers were men, who didn't actually cook, it was often a hit-or-miss proposition.

The kitchen of this 1905 Julia Morgan–designed home in Berkeley was re-done by someone even more obsessive than myself—and that's saying something. The vintage refrigerator has been installed in a custom tiled enclosure. Milk-glass doors with nickel-plated frames make up the front of the refrigerator. Above the fridge, tiled recesses are used for display. At one end, a 1912 Universal combination fuel stove backs up to the enclosure under a massive plaster stove hood. At the other end, though it can't be seen in the photo, is a tiled niche for the telephone. Hanging reproduction light fixtures (the "Burnside" from Rejuvenation in Portland, Oregon) are fitted with reproduction Edison bulbs. In the right foreground is one end of the tiled sink counter, which features a raised dishwasher hidden by a tiled and nickel-plated front that matches the fridge. At the far end of the room, an oak secretary holds cookbooks.

ABOVE: At one end of a new kitchen in a 1909 bungalow in Seattle, a generously sized breakfast nook has been built into a corner under a bank of (new) windows that look out into the trees of the wooded lot. The L-shaped bench is paired with an oak trestle table and can seat more than your average breakfast nook. A four-arm chandelier with art-glass shades hangs over the table, which is set with Arts and Crafts china on embroidered linen place mats.

OPPOSITE: The kitchen of the guest quarters in the same 1905 home has a look of indeterminate vintage. While the counter and floor tile, as well as the milk-glass-and-brass fronts on the lower cabinets (which hide various appliances) evoke the 1920s, the upper cabinets with their glass shelving and sliding glass doors are reminiscent of a somewhat later era. The cooktop and wall oven (though it's not exactly on the wall) are obviously of the current century. Subway-tiled walls and more utilitarian fixtures could have been there in 1905, though these are actually new.

ABOVE: Though this late-Victorian home is not a bungalow, its kitchen is definitely a bungalow kitchen. Lacking the continuous countertops that we now take for granted, it has only one built-in cupboard (often called a kitchen dresser) and a freestanding Spark stove, probably from the 1920s or early 1930s. A worktable (tarted up for the photo) is centered under the most fabulous thing in the room, a still-functioning combination gas and electric light fixture (note the flames). Combination fixtures were a bad idea on so many levels, but isn't it cool to see one that still works?

OPPOSITE: One belief that carried over to bungalows from the Victorians was an obsession with sanitation, for which there were good reasons at the time. There was an idea that food should not be prepared in the same room where the dirty dishes were washed, which lead to this-the scullery. In many bungalows, the sink is in a separate room off the main kitchen, as this one is. The area beneath the sink was open to allow for ventilation. Electricity was a new thing as well, so there was conspicuous display of the new technology (the equivalent of having a plasma-screen TV today), thus, the bare light bulb on a cord. The paint-spatter linoleum on the floor dates to the 1950s. For more information on these subjects, I'm afraid you will just have to buy our other books, *Bungalow Kitchens* and *Linoleum*, which go into far more detail than there is room for here.

ABOVE: The kitchen in this Seattle bungalow was built by the homeowner, using (appropriately enough) a Craftsman table saw. The cabinets have beadboard insets in their frame-and-panel doors that match the wainscoating that runs all the way around the room. The doors fasten with brass cupboard catches. The cabinets, the trim, and the floor are all Douglas fir. A one-bowl porcelain–over–cast-iron sink with a vintage wall-mounted faucet is flanked by hexagonal-tile counters. The cabinets have no toe kick, unlike modern cabinets. The pegged joints of the door and window casings (original to the house) are mirrored by similar joints in the shallow glass-doored cabinet over the oak table and chairs. As is proper, the vintage light fixtures aren't on a wall switch—they have pull chains and square turn-switches on the sockets. On the right, a General Electric Monitortop refrigerator (introduced in 1927) stands next to a nickel-plated wall sconce. The walls are painted the kind of yellowish color that the original, probably cream-colored, paint would have oxidized to after eighty or so years. All of the packages in the shallow cabinet are vintage. There is no dishwasher. I want to sit down in this kitchen and eat cookies and lemonade.

LEFT: Several decades are happening at once in this kitchen: the home is of the Victorian era; the Wedgewood combination stove is from the 1930s; the paint-spatter linoleum is from the 1950s; and as for the Campbell's "M'm! M'm! Good!" apron—well, one hesitates to speculate on that. The whole room is lined in beadboard (narrow tongue-and-groove paneling), as was often the case in bungalows as well.

LEFT: At the Patterson House in Fremont, California, the kitchen was remodeled in 1915. They bought the latest wood-burning Wedgewood stove, cast iron with nickel plating, and next to it they put their new Ruud instantaneous water heater, also cast iron, its Arts and Crafts decoration picked out in gold. In our day, no attempt would be made to beautify a water heater.

The kitchen of the 1908 Bennett House in Lake Forest, California, shows off the sort of kitchen Stickley might have been talking about, with an abundance of cupboards, drawers, and tilt-out bins. In the foreground, a Monitortop refrigerator has its own niche. At the far end of the room is a 1920s Hotpoint electric stove. All this sits on a floor of easy-to-clean blue marbleized linoleum.

OPPOSITE: A porcelain sink on legs with separate taps for hot and cold water stands ready for washing-up chores at the Lanterman House in La Cañada-Flintridge, California. A very sanitary hexagonal-tile floor and subway-tile wainscoting make the room easy to keep clean, although generally only the fairly wealthy could afford a tile floor in the kitchen. Others made do with wood and linoleum.

CLEANLINESS IS NEXT TO GODLINESS

Indoor plumbing is the very basis of modern civilization and likely the one thing about it most of us would be unwilling to give up. Conveniently, plumbing was pretty much perfected in the nineteenth century, and the bathroom in a bungalow is still entirely functional even by twenty first century standards. At the time bungalows were being built, the key words in bathrooms were "sanitary, white, and clean." People were worried about germs. According to the Standard Sanitary Manufacturing Company, "Money cannot be invested to better advantage than in a sure source of

health and convenience to the entire household…No other part of the house possesses the charm peculiar to the ideally equipped bathroom." Later on, in the 1920s, colored tile and fixtures began to make an appearance, after the realization that germs were colorblind.

The general number of bathrooms in a two- or three-bedroom bungalow was one. (Remember, these people were still pretty excited about having indoor plumbing at all.) If you were really lucky, there might be a half bath off the kitchen or the utility porch, or maybe an extra sink installed in a bedroom.

Even the maid gets a nice-looking bathroom in a home in the West Adams district of Los Angeles. A tile-in tub is set into an arched niche, while three different colors of green tile decorate the walls and floor. The toilet uses a pressure-flush valve rather than a tank; this kind of toilet is usually seen in public restrooms or large apartment buildings rather than residences, the reason being that this kind of valve not only saves water but allows for serial flushing without waiting for the tank to refill.

Part of an addition by the second owners of Artemisia, a colorful tiled bath with a stunning sunken shower (beyond the two arches) uses mint green and burgundy tiles with a decorative leaf border and four-inch hexagonal floor tiles. These kinds of outrageous color combinations were typical of 1920s and 1930s bathrooms, though many were still white, of course. A white sink basin is mounted under a black marble slab set on a filigreed base with a green finish that matches the sconces above.

LEFT: Another of the Riordan House bathrooms has a slightly shorter claw-foot tub, a rounded rather than rectangular shelf under its medicine cabinet, but the same battleship linoleum floor. For some reason the towel bars are not mounted on the molding in this bath. The round wall-hung sink is just to the left of the tub.

OPPOSITE: The Riordan House in Flagstaff had seven bathrooms, a lot for 1904, when it was built. They were all as white and sanitary as this one, with its long claw-foot tub (the double-wall tub that we are familiar with wasn't invented until 1911), enameled walls, and gray battleship linoleum floor (yes, they really did use it on battleships!). There is only a simple four-inch molding run around the room at eye level- mostly for mounting the towel bars.

A double wall tub in a subway-tiled enclosure is a classic bungalow bathroom feature. Porcelain cross-handled faucets and a nickel-plated tub spout are also traditional. In fact, nickel-plated everything was pretty much the deal.

A nickel-plated ring shower with its own separate faucets is mounted at one end of a Roman tub in the Lanterman House in La Cañada-Flintridge, California. The tub faucets are centered on the edge of the tub, and the tub spout is that little round thingy halfway down the inside. The subway-tile wainscoting is capped with a small molding, and above that is a hand-painted mural of irises. Two-inch hexagonal tiles cover the floor. Two-inch tiles were less common than the ubiquitous one-inch hexagons found in so many bungalows.

ABOVE: Elaborate art tile covers the sides of a blue tile-in tub in a 1929 home in Los Angeles. A companion border tops the wainscoating, and the green four-by-four-inch floor tile is laid on the diagonal inside a rectangular border.

LEFT: The problem with claw-foot tubs is that dirt tends to collect underneath and behind them, and it's hard to get to. This, of course, is not sanitary, so someone came up with the pedestal tub. This version, at Manka's Lodge, a bed and breakfast in Inverness, California, is a Roman tub (round at both ends) with a wall-mounted nickel-plated faucet. The bathroom walls are covered with painted board-and-batten paneling, and linoleum tile with an inlaid border covers the floor. Next to the tub, a painted metal cabinet on legs holds towels and toiletries.

Art-tile bathrooms are found in later bungalows, generally those built in the late 1920s or 1930s, after the heyday of the Arts and Crafts Movement. Most bungalows built from 1900–16, generally the agreed-upon glory days of Arts and Crafts, would have had all-white, sanitary bathrooms (maybe a hint of color in a decorative tile border, but not much else). This particular home in Ventura, California, has a bathroom entirely outfitted in burgundy and black Malibu tile. The curved corner shower, shown here in close-up, has a distinctive pierced flower tile that covers the shower drain.

The toilet was often installed in a separate space, known as a water closet, a civilized feature that is currently enjoying a ren-aissance in new homes. Except for the unusual wooden tank, this is the classic wash-down toi-let found in a huge majority of bungalows: a wall-hung tank that connects to the bowl with an L-shaped pipe. A wash-down toilet can be recognized by the distinctive bump on the front of the bowl, which has to do with the shape of the trap. Conveniently for bungalow own-ers, reproductions of these toi-lets, modified to be low-flow (the originals use six or seven gal-lons per flush) are starting to become available. For more arcane facts about toilets, you'll just have to purchase our book, *Bungalow Bathrooms*.

RIGHT: Sinks in bungalows tended to be either pedestal or wall-hung for the most part. (That's wall-hung, not well-hung). Plumbing changes very slowly, so there may be little difference between a sink from 1905, 1915, or 1925. This sink, at the Lanterman House is oval and rests on a somewhat classical-looking base. Separate hot and cold taps were the norm for bathroom sinks until the 1930s, when mixing faucets began to be used. Which is weird, since mixing faucets were used on tubs, showers, and kitchen sinks going back to the late-nineteenth century. Many kinds of custom hardware were manufactured for bathrooms, including toothbrush holders (in center), cup holders (at left with liquid soap dispenser), shelf brackets, and, of course, towel bars and hooks, toilet paper holders, etc.

By the late 1920s and 1930s, it was literally "anything goes," as amply demonstrated here in a 1931 bath in San Francisco. Who knew that cornflower-blue fixtures went with lavender, cobalt, yellow, and chartreuse tiles and a gold metallic ceiling? The nickel-plated shower door is typical for stall showers even earlier than this.

REST AND REPOSE

In the bungalow, the function of the bedroom was primarily sleep. Therefore, everything was designed to be calm and soothing. Although the woodwork was often left natural in the bedrooms as well, the wall colors were usually more delicate than in the formal rooms, and sometimes the woodwork was painted. Closets were generally small because people had fewer clothes than we do now. Some closets had built-in chests of drawers, obviating the need for a dresser.

Many bungalows also had sleeping porches. The fad for sleeping outside, even in winter, had much to do with tuberculosis. Antibiotics not having been synthesized yet (Streptomycin wasn't introduced until 1943), the only cure available was fresh air and rest. Usually sleeping porches were off the bedroom, making it easy to drag the bed outside, though sometimes due to the house's design they were off a hallway or some other room. Some were completely open, though commonly roofed, while others were glassed or screened in with sashes that opened, folded, or slid. No doubt it was pleasant to sleep out of doors on warm summer evenings, but to do it in winter takes a strength of character we now lack. Also, the increased noise of modern life has made it more problematic to sleep outside, even if one desires to do so.

Rustic accessories and a pine bed give an informal look to a bungalow bedroom in Victoria, British Columbia. Twig tables with deer-foot lamps (I find these a little disturbing, personally) on both sides of the bed provide storage for needed items. A simple off-white chenille bedspread contrasts with embroidered souvenir pillows from Yosemite and Smoky Mountains National Parks (no, I don't know why they're not from Canadian parks), as well as a leather pillow. A tapestry of a stag hangs above the bed. On the right, four paintings hang from a brass curtain rod, there being no picture molding.

Mottled walls in a soft green color harmonize with an exquisite bedspread appliquéd with pansies in the master bedroom of a Seattle bungalow. The tones of the slatted oak bed and matching nightstands pick up the caramel color of some of the pansies. An Arts and Crafts rocker in a similar tone anchors the corner by the window. The floors are Douglas fir, their reddish tones picked up by the cedar chest used for storage at the end of the bed. Bedroom woodwork was often painted, though not always, and often pastel colors were used in the bedrooms rather than the more earthy tones that were found in the formal rooms.

Brass or other metal beds were popular, as they were considered sanitary. (You have no idea how obsessed these people were with sanitation. Possibly with good reason—antibiotics weren't discovered till 1928 and weren't available to the general public until World War II.) This one has a simple quilt that shows off a collection of cat-themed pillows done in punch-needle embroidery. Oak night tables with turned legs flank the bed, with electrified kerosene lamps for lighting, and a late-Victorian dresser and mirror (it's kinda Arts and Crafts–looking on the side) sits next to a door leading to the bathroom that one can't get into, there being a chair in front of it. (Big argument with photographer about this—I lost.) Four-light chandeliers were not common in bedrooms—two lights being more likely.

The carved floral design of the oak bed in the guest room of this Seattle bungalow is mirrored by a similar design in the Bradbury and Bradbury wallpaper, and in the embroidery of the linen pillow. A woven bedspread in a tulip design picks up the wallpaper colors. A green wicker desk and chair furnishes a place for guests to write correspondence. Okay, probably answer e-mail on their laptop, but "correspondence" sounds so genteel. A mirror in a copper repoussé frame hangs on the wall above the desk.

Round-top windows on two sides of a bedroom in a Seattle bungalow give a feeling of sleeping in the treetops, with a view of a wooded area across the road. The bed is made up with a simple quilt and tapestry shams. A bowl fixture hangs from brass rods over the bed. Simple café curtains allow the view to be seen from the bed while still maintaining privacy.

A contemporary Arts and Crafts bed with burl-wood panels interspersed among the slats is set under high windows with simple muslin tab curtains on black iron rods. Narrow tongue-and-groove paneling can be glimpsed between the painted ceiling beams. The bed is dressed in quilted and matelassé linens in earthy tones of taupe, sage, and white.

RIGHT: Artemisia in Hollywood has just about the best sleeping porch I've ever seen, as well as the biggest. L-shaped, it wraps around the back of the house and has five built-in Murphy beds. Three of them are shown here—the corbels become the legs when the beds are opened.

OPPOSITE: A fireplace in a bedroom, especially the master bedroom, was a feature in some bungalows. The bedroom of this southern California bungalow is new construction, though it has the same gray-stained redwood paneling as some of the original parts of the house. A new fireplace is faced with contemporary tile by tilemaker Laird Plumleigh, though the "X" tiles in the center are vintage Grueby tiles. Above the fireplace, more Grueby tiles are framed as art (with one Rookwood tile in the center) Narrow book-shelves, niches for display, and a bench are all built in to the fireplace surround. The cathedral ceiling mirrors a simi-lar ceiling in the living room. Owl andirons with glass eyes that glow are antique, though similar ones are now being produced. An Arts and Crafts rocker by Charles Stickley provides a comfortable place to watch the fire.

Built-in furniture like this chest of drawers tucked into a window nook in a Victoria, British Columbia, bungalow were a feature in some bedrooms. More often a chest of drawers was built in to a closet, which would still be considered a civilized feature today. Two light sconces are placed on either side of the window, and a simple bed and desk complete the furnishings. Bedroom woodwork was more likely to be painted than the woodwork in the formal rooms, which doesn't make it okay to paint yours if it isn't currently painted.

ABOVE: The upstairs rooms of the Duncan-Irwin House in Pasadena are connected by a covered outdoor walkway overlooking the atrium and fountain in the center of the house. A simple trellis covers the center, providing dappled shade in the daylight. The walkway is deep enough to serve as a porch, and is outfitted with wicker furniture in various seating areas. What is difficult to convey, even with Linda's very fine photography, is how magical it feels to be there.

LEFT: In one of the bedrooms of the 1905 Wadsworth House in Berkeley, architect Julia Morgan opted for stained redwood woodwork and a textured wall covering. The Stickley Brothers slatted bed has been placed in the middle of the room facing the windows, which have a lovely view into the trees. Behind the bed, a wooden screen (with an added stencil by designer Helen Foster) provides some privacy from the door.

WOMEN'S WORK

Somewhat larger bungalows may have had extra rooms whose function was not chiseled in concrete. Often these were used as sewing rooms, as nurseries for infants, as playrooms for the children, or as guest rooms. Some were essentially a nook off a hallway, while others were simply small rooms.

Middle class women were, of course, expected to stay home and take care of the children and the house. This was deemed to be their highest calling. Men were expected to work outside the home, and much of how the bungalow was set up was to make it comfortable for them when they arrived home from a hard day at work. Still, it was generally an eight-hour day. Nowadays, women are also expected to work outside the home, and still take care of the children and the house. Strides have been made, but we have a ways to go on that front. And the eight-hour day, and the forty-hour week, has now turned into the twelve-hour day and the eighty-hour week, either from the job or from the commute. On that front we appear to be sliding backwards. And we are the only first-world country that does not offer health care to all its citizens.

OTHER SPACES

Bungalow floor plans often saved spaced by eliminating hallways, or at least making them very short. This means that often the bedrooms open directly off some other room—the dining room, the kitchen, the entry hall, even the living room. That was part of the informality as well. The bathroom, and often there was only one, could either be placed between two bedrooms, accessible only from the bedrooms, or provision might be made for a short hallway, so that it could be accessed from the public parts of the house. In a less well-designed bungalow, it might open directly off the kitchen, dining room, or even the living room.

The stairway necessary to reach the upper floor of a one and a half story bungalow was normally made an architectural feature of the room, screened with spindles or some other kind of woodwork. In a larger bungalow, it might start in the entry hall, which would be larger than normal, more like a reception hall, and one or more landings might be included.

A bay windowed room on the first floor of the Duncan-Irwin House can be closed off with a pocket door and has been set up as a nursery. An antique oak crib is set up in front of the windows, and nearby, a round table with a mica-shaded wicker lamp. The windows have linen scrim curtains to filter the light. Through the window, two of the home's clinker brick–and–arroyo stone pillars are visible.

A leather-upholstered Monterey settle provides suitable accompaniment to the cowboy art hanging above the paneling. French doors with wide muntins lead into the dining room beyond, flanked by two flared lanterns.

If there was an inside stairway to the basement (if there was a basement at all), it generally would start from the kitchen, back hall, or utility porch, although occasionally a basement stair would start from the entry hall, or the bedroom hall, if there was one. In areas where basements were common, they were often made into living space, having a fireplace, possibly a paneled room—a forerunner of the "rumpus room" which has now morphed into the "family room."

In the back of the bungalow, or sometimes on the side, there was usually a utility porch (sometimes called a "kitchen porch" at the time). This was the location for the laundry, unless it was in the basement, as well as a typical place for the icebox. The porch might be glassed-in or merely screened. Sometimes it was nothing more than a back hallway. This is where bungalow designers often fell down on the whole "interpenetration of indoor and outdoor spaces." In most bungalows, the way to the backyard is through the utility porch. In part, this is because the back yard was considered more of a utility space, used for clothes drying and the vegetable garden, and the front (or side) garden was more formal.

The pipes for the pipe organ at Artemisia are hidden behind two sets of bi-fold doors in the upstairs hallway with elaborately scrolled insets and a really lovely grain pattern. As is obvious from the turned balusters and carved newel post, Artemisia isn't all Arts and Crafts on the inside, whatever the outside may be. And at 10,000 square feet, it's not exactly a tiny bungalow, either—though it did make my own home, at a mere 3,800 square feet, seem like a tiny cottage. I can say without fear of contradiction that pipe organs were not common in bungalows.

In case you thought the two-story living room was just some modern tract-home aberration, here's proof to the contrary. Walk through the front door of this Berkeley Arts and Crafts home by architect/builder Leola Hall and find yourself in this soaring space. Paneled in Douglas fir with insets of veneer and lit by beveled-glass windows, it's a symphony in wood. The stepped pattern of the stair railing, with its square balusters, leads the eye upward. A small balcony is cantilevered out over the beveled French doors below that lead to the dining room. On the ceiling, beams whose triangular profiles are highlighted by the molding that encases the ends show how beautiful expressed structure can be. The vertical uprights of the wall paneling are balanced by three wide horizontal boards at intervals. Between the ceiling beams, wide boards with chamfered (cut at an angle) edges provide a repeating pattern down the length of the room. Mica-shaded lanterns hang from large wooden brackets. On the floor, the narrower-than-usual oak boards offer an interesting contrast to the rest of the woodwork.

Though appearing simple at first glance, the stairway of Greene and Greene's Bolton House reveals more complexity as you study it. The pattern of the alternating wide and narrow balusters (each step has one of each) is balanced by the board-and-batten paneling of the opposite side. The front profile of each tread continues as a pegged molding along the side, which extends the horizontal plane of each step. The bottom step wraps around the side of the newel post in an expansive way. In the entry, a tile-top oak table with slightly splayed legs and pegged through-tenons holding the lower shelf shows the same swirled grain as the quarter-sawn stair treads. Leaded glass (designed by Charles) enhances the front door and its overhead transom.

ABOVE: Stepped baluster sections with square spindles and four-by-four-inch newel posts screen the staircase at one end of the living room in this Berkeley home by architect/builder Leola Hall. Redwood board-and-batten paneling continues the line of the built-out top on the clinker-brick fireplace. A Morris chair and ottoman sits in the corner next to the built-in bookcase, with a small hexagonal side table and a contemporary mica-shaded lamp.

OPPOSITE: The staircase of the Duncan-Irwin House is more enclosed than some of the other Greene and Greene staircases, though slits in the lower paneled wall and a screen of alternating wide and narrow boards allow light to come through. The staircase is lined with very narrow casement windows that are constructed with pegged joinery, and include what is possibly the world's tiniest casement window, just above the landing. It's diminutive size is only emphasized by the very long top casing above it. Note how the top casing of the lower casement is slightly higher than the horizontal trim of the paneling on either side—the kind of subtle detail that isn't obvious at first glance. In the hallway below, a green art-glass lantern is suspended from an elaborate wooden canopy. The door to the closet under the stairs has delicate stepped detailing in its crosspieces.

To the right of the front door as you enter the Gould House in Ventura, California, the simple staircase designed by Henry Greene ascends to the second floor. Henry had a more restrained and straight-lined style than his brother, Charles, and the simplicity of the architecture here is appropriate to what was essentially a farmhouse. Yet the tops of the posts were carved with a simple design of a rectangle with corner squares, and each post has a small corbel. A large casement window that matches others in the house floods the landing with light. On the landing, a shallow niche with a small platform and drawer below contains a mirror designed by Henry and sconces on either side, the whole thing reminiscent of a Japanese *tokonama* (alcove).

□ STEWARDSHIP □

IS MONEY TO BE GATHERED? CUT DOWN THE PLEASANT TREES AMONG
THE HOUSES, PULL DOWN ANCIENT AND VENERABLE BUILDINGS FOR THE
MONEY THAT A FEW SQUARE YARDS OF LONDON DIRT WILL FETCH;
BLACKEN RIVERS, HIDE THE SUN AND POISON THE AIR WITH SMOKE AND
WORSE, AND IT'S NOBODY'S BUSINESS TO SEE TO IT OR MEND IT:
THAT IS ALL THAT MODERN COMMERCE, THE COUNTING-HOUSE FORGETFUL
OF THE WORKSHOP, WILL DO FOR US HEREIN.

W I L L I A M   M O R R I S

As mentioned previously, William Morris was also a historic preservationist. In
1877, he founded the Society for the Protection of Ancient Buildings, an organization
that is still in existence. In the above quote, he kind of hit the nail on the head. Historic
buildings continue to be pulled down, manufacturing continues to poison the environment, old-growth trees are clear-cut, and farmland paved over, all in the name of profit.
In every town, there are and have been property owners or developers or city councils
or bureaucrats or colleges or businesses perfectly willing to demolish one bungalow or
a hundred in the name of "progress."

All shingles and redwood, the exterior of Artemisia in Hollywood is pure southern California Arts and Crafts. A series of double knee braces under the roof overhangs pairs with notched rafter tails, while the planter boxes under the windows are supported by more brackets. In the gable at far left, a complex series of outriggers that may even be structural adorn the gable end, which also has numerous beam ends piercing its fascia board. The front terraces are composed of brick and quarry tile. On the right, a brick column has a leaded-glass light fixture set into it as part of the structure. Barely seen on the lower terrace are doors that lead to the ballroom on the lower level. Most bungalows didn't have ballrooms either, but, then, this isn't exactly a bungalow, for all that it's an extremely fabulous house.

These are the original garage doors of the tower bungalow, still with their original hardware. Above the doors, half-timbering with pebble-dash infill (and those are some really big pebbles!) awaits restoration.

A bungalow like this one in Vancouver, B.C., would be considered a tear-down in many cities (possibly including Vancouver) simply because it is a little run-down and in need of some work. But if you can look beyond that, you can see how fabulous it is, with its curved wraparound porch supported by bulbous columns, its interesting roofline and dormer (did it have windows once and someone covered them up with stucco?), and, of course, a really cool tower.

Most buildings built for the middle or working classes, like this Chicago bungalow (look at the fabulous two-tone brick and gold-accented art glass) were not even taken seriously until quite recently, and still aren't in most places. Chicago has made great strides in saving its bungalows through education and low-cost loans for restoration through the Historic Chicago Bungalow Initiative.

That the bungalows pictured in this book are still here to be photographed means that they were preserved. They were not bulldozed to make way for parking lots or office buildings or strip malls or mini-mansions. They did not have all of their historic fabric removed in order to install the latest fad in décor or architecture from some decade or other, or if they did, someone took the trouble to restore them back to what they once were and what they were supposed to be.

In most places, bungalows aren't even considered to be historic or worth preserving. They are rarely protected by law, even in cities and towns that may have some kind of historic preservation regulations or guidelines. (The majority of towns and cities have nothing.) They are regarded by many people as little more than shacks. Their only protection comes from caring and knowledgeable owners. But it is not enough to care for your own house; you have to care for your neighborhood and your community.

Even houses by architectural icons like Frank Lloyd Wright have been demolished in the name of progress or profit (and these two are usually hopelessly intertwined). The ones that remain, like Oak Park's 1902 Heurtley House, shown here, are the legacy of caring owners.

I believe it is time for a new kind of historic preservation. Up until now, the mainstream preservation movement has concerned itself with what could be termed "trophy buildings;" city halls, courthouses, mansions, historic theatres, hotels, residences designed by famous architects, etc. All of these are eminently worth preserving. But while those buildings were being fought for, thousands of more modest buildings were lost to the wrecking ball, and continue to be lost. Few people have stepped up to defend the Arts and Crafts bungalows, working class Victorians, historic gas stations, small commercial buildings, old warehouses, and other modest buildings. A huge number of them have been demolished. Those buildings represent a large part of our history, the history of ordinary people who built them, worked in them, lived in them—that is our real history, not the history of wars and politicians and great events. We are told this is the price of progress. It isn't. As Russell Baker said, "Usually, terrible things that are done with the excuse that progress requires them are not really progress at all, but just terrible things."

And we can no longer afford to throw away the now irreplaceable materials and craftsmanship that went into those buildings. To do so is an affront to the labor and

Opponents of preservation often use the phrase, "It's just an old house, it's nothing special." It makes me want to hit them. Even people who are supposedly preservationists will say things like, "Well, they were cheaply built." This shows a lack of understanding of the word "cheap" at the time versus how the same word is viewed today. Today's "cheap construction" really *is* shoddy, using inferior materials that don't last. Actually, today that's true even of high-end construction. In the past, cheap merely meant inexpensive, and didn't have the negative connotations we now attach to it. I consider this modest bungalow in Los Angeles to be as worthy of preservation as a gigantic house built for some rich people during the same year. I don't believe it is an either/or proposition.

Preserving an icon like the Duncan-Irwin House, shown here, is a fairly easy argument. Yet this house was preserved and restored by sensitive owners, not by the City of Pasadena. Although the city passed the Blacker Ordinance after the rape of Greene and Greene's Blacker House by a Texas antiques dealer, it is one of the few places in the country with any kind of legislation in place to protect historic interiors. Traditional designations like the National Register of Historic Places, or various kinds of landmark designations, protect only the exterior.

ABOVE: In no way am I saying that "trophy buildings" shouldn't be saved. The Gamble House, one of Greene and Greene's masterpieces, could certainly be considered a trophy building. But nonetheless, it only became a house museum because Mrs. Gamble was horrified to overhear a potential buyer say they would have to paint all the woodwork, causing her to change her mind about selling and give it to the City of Pasadena and the University of Southern California (joint custody) instead. Even that was only possible because she didn't need the money. Thus some of Charles and Henry's artistry has been preserved for all of us.

OPPOSITE: It's not the Gamble House, but the wisteria-patterned art glass of this Pasadena front door and its sidelights certainly takes some inspiration from there. A reproduction lantern hangs on one side over the ubiquitous Dard Hunter doormat which no self-respecting Arts and Crafts home should be without.

artistry of those who built them. These buildings ARE the old growth forests we cut down, the stones we quarried, the metals we mined, and the bricks we fired. The tiniest bungalow contains several hundred board feet of old growth timber—it is an insult to the trees that gave their lives to send that wood splintered and useless to a landfill.

I believe it is time for a new kind of historic preservation, a radical kind of preservation that adheres to these principles:

1. All historic buildings are created equal and endowed by their creators with the inalienable right to remain standing, be properly maintained, and not be sacrificed on a whim, be that the whim of an individual, a government, an institution, or a corporation.

2. Historic buildings should not be sacrificed in the name of "economic development," which is almost always a code word for "profit" or "power."

3. That "smart growth" which demolishes historic buildings and replaces them with

inappropriately dense "infill" is not smart at all, and will eventually be discredited.

4. There is no connection whatsoever between building more density in urban cores (at the expense of historic buildings) and the paving of farmland—both are driven by the pursuit of profit and nothing else.

5. Ninety-nine percent of contemporary architecture sucks.

6. There is no bigger scam than vinyl window replacement.

7. "Not in My Backyard" (NIMBY) really stands for Not Intimidated Much By Yelling.

8. Historic buildings are not to blame for whatever social ills may be associated with them. The building did not choose to become a drug house or to have irresponsible owners.

9. To paraphrase a Buddhist motto: No matter how innumerable historic buildings are, we vow to save them all.

I propose to call this new kind of preservation the Historic Architecture Liberation Front. H.A.L.F. has no structure, no board of directors, no non-profit status, no membership fee. There are no by-laws, and if you don't like the principles above you can make up your own. There is no leadership. Anyone who wants to save historic buildings can belong. Mainstream preservationists can join under assumed names. Anyone can

Though modest, a cross-gabled bungalow in Eagle Rock, California, has its own charms, from the square purlins "piercing" the fascia board to the art-glass and corbeled shelf on the front door. You can be sure, for all its modesty, that it's better than whatever might replace it.

start their own chapter and call it whatever they want. The most important thing is to fight for historic buildings. All of them. Using whatever means you can think of: persuasion,

LEFT: A Los Angeles bungalow sports interesting stepped windows in the main gable, as well as a plethora of sculpted beam ends and knee braces. Stone pillars support the porch roof.

BELOW: Unique stonework makes up most of this Denver bungalow, except for the shingles in the gables, but my favorite thing is the porte cochere over the sidewalk (the driveway is on the other side). This kind of zaniness is rarely duplicated in a modern building.

ABOVE: Except for the aluminum soffit replacement, this multicolored brick bungalow in Chicago is intact right down to its front planter box. Chicago bungalows are already quite densely packed; if you look closely just to the left of the dormer, you can see the side gable of the house next-door. Bungalow neighborhoods traditionally have all the features now espoused by "the new urbanism", like density, access to transit, walkability, front porches, etc. Let's just call it "the old urbanism" and not destroy it because of some city planners' need to prove they're up on the latest theory. Remember, these are the same people who brought us "urban renewal," which destroyed hundreds of thousands of historic buildings and decimated neighborhoods nationwide. In ten years, "smart growth" will be renounced by planners in the same way that urban renewal is now.

LEFT: Just look at the swooping side gable and upturned ends on the fascia boards on this Milwaukee bungalow—how cool is that? Not to mention the fish-scale shingles on the flared dormer. Look at all the bricks and limestone accents. Do you know the biggest component of landfills nationwide is construction and demolition debris? Never mind recycling aluminum cans—stop tearing down houses instead.

lawsuits, humor, non-violent demonstrations, websites, letter-writing campaigns, political action, education, tours, pranks, documentaries, buying the building, becoming a historic district, applying for grants, running for mayor—whatever it takes.

The destruction of historic buildings robs us all of something important. It is theft, pure and simple. It may be disguised with lofty pronouncements about bettering the community or that it will achieve some praiseworthy goal, but it is still theft. Morris was aware of this:

> "Look at the houses (there are plenty to choose from)! I will not say, are they beautiful, for you say you don't care whether they are or not: but just look at the wretched pennyworths of material, of accommodation, of ornament doled out to you! if there were one touch of generosity, of honest pride, of wish to please about them, I would forgive them in the lump. But there is none—not one.
>
> It is for this that you have sacrificed your cedars and planes and may-trees, which I do believe you really liked—are you satisfied?
>
> Indeed you cannot be: all you can do is to go to your business, converse with your family, eat, drink, and sleep, and try to forget it, but whenever you think of it, you will admit that a loss without compensation has befallen you and your neighbours."

Keep in mind at all times that you are a caretaker for your house, a curator, if you will—the house was there before you, and if it is lucky, it will be there after you are gone. Think carefully about what you do, try to remember that the universe does not revolve around you, and try not to do anything that some later owner will be cursing you for, as you may be cursing some previous owner right now. (Maybe that's why they're called P.O.s—because the things they did make you P.O.'d.)

Anyone who has ever laid bricks could tell you how much labor went into even a smallish brick bungalow with a simple bond pattern like this one in Denver. Or the wood inside and outside, much of it sawn by hand. Who are we to destroy what others labored to build?

NEWS FROM SOMEWHERE

YES, SURELY! AND IF OTHERS CAN SEE IT AS I HAVE SEEN IT, THEN IT MAY BE CALLED A VISION RATHER THAN A DREAM.

WILLIAM MORRIS,
NEWS FROM NOWHERE

It's been seventeen years since I wandered down the Arts and Crafts path by purchasing a 1912 bungalow. It wasn't my intention. My only intention was to buy an old house. It's just that here in the East Bay, as the Berkeley-Oakland side of the San Francisco Bay is called, there are a lot of bungalows. I looked at 150 houses (and, yes, I still have all the flyers) and probably one hundred of them were bungalows. They began to work their slow magic. By the time I walked into the one I eventually bought, I was hooked and I didn't even know it. I loved the leaded glass doors of its china cabinet and bookcases. I loved the arched opening of its cast-stone fireplace. Those were the immediate things. As I lived there, other, more subtle things wormed their way into my consciousness: the Douglas fir woodwork with its darkened and alligatored shellac, the nine-foot ceilings that felt so much better than the eight-foot ceilings I grew up with,

To my knowledge, there weren't any Spanish missions in Milwaukee, which makes the Mission-style gables and red-tile roof of this bungalow all the more amusing. Well, maybe they're Dutch gables. It's still amusing.

Several bungalows later, I found the house of my dreams, the unbelievable 1905 Sunset House. Linda took this picture of the living room on the day I moved in two years ago. This is my freestanding, asymmetrical, clinker-brick fireplace. Behind it there's a bench flanked by bookcases with sliding doors. The firebox doesn't open to the back, so all there is to look at from the bench is the back of the fireplace, an oversight on the part of the designer, if you ask me. The trusses really are structural—in fact, the fireplace itself is structural. The cheap home-center chandeliers will be removed eventually. To the left (not shown), the floor steps up six inches to a large sunroom, which also makes an excellent stage for musical performances. The whole room is thirty-seven feet long and seventeen feet wide, not counting the area behind the fireplace. There are casement windows on all four sides of the room. This photo was taken with professional photography lighting. Never again do I want anyone to complain to me that their bungalow is dark—you people don't know from darkness. I love my house.

the patina of the brass door hardware. It just felt like home. It spoke to me. Nine houses later, bungalows still speak to me. To fix them and to write of them has become my life's work. I find them endlessly fascinating, and even after all this time, they can still surprise me.

It was not as though I'd never lived in an old house before. In Detroit, where I was born, my family had a half-timbered Tudor Revival house. Later, in Indianapolis, we had a 1920s gambrel-roofed Colonial. Although when we moved to California we lived in a ranch house, whose only relation to bungalows was its one story and exposed rafters. After I left home, I lived in old houses—often ones that had been divided up into apartments—one was even a bungalow. But they were all painted white. Until I saw ones that weren't, I hadn't really experienced the artistic whole that a bungalow is meant to be.

> NINE HOUSES LATER, BUNGALOWS STILL SPEAK TO ME. TO FIX THEM AND TO WRITE OF THEM HAS BECOME MY LIFE'S WORK.

I didn't grow up with Arts and Crafts stuff. There was no Morris chair passed down from my grandparents. We had some art pottery because my parents grew up in Ohio, and probably everybody in Ohio had some piece of Rookwood or Roseville or some unsigned vase from a Zanesville pottery. We had two Van Briggle pieces—a tall turquoise vase and bowl with pine cones on it. I loved them as a child, and still do.

Apparently unlike many other people, my parents weren't apt to redecorate the house as each new style came along. Possibly from being children of the Depression, and also because my mother had taste, they bought fairly simple, well-made furniture and kept it forever. Some of it got reupholstered or refinished as necessary. I still have the couch they bought when they got married in 1940, and now, since my mother passed away and my father moved into a condo, I also have the Shaker style dining set they had built by a craftsman in the hills of Tennessee. The simple style of it looks fine in a bungalow.

Though there were not many Arts and Crafts things around me, Arts and Crafts principles were another story. My sisters and I learned to make things. We always had what I would call "art toys"—things that made designs. I had an artistic bent, and it was encouraged with art supplies, and later, painting lessons. My mother taught me to embroider, a skill I still enjoy. She also taught me to paint rooms—I started when I was eleven. I learned to sew. From my father I learned to fix things and use tools. I am always thankful that I had no brothers, because maybe he would have taught these things to the boys and not the girls, as is often the way. But he had no one to teach his skills to but girls, so he taught them to the three of us. It always surprised me when

other girls didn't know how to fix flat tires on their bikes or stop a toilet from running. Many Sundays after church we would go out to look at model homes in the new subdivisions being built around Indianapolis. To this day I like to go out to open houses on Sundays, though now they're old houses instead of new ones.

Given all this, it's not altogether surprising that all three of us went to college and now have design degrees. My older sister became a potter. My younger sister became a jeweler. I became a maker of clothing. Interestingly enough, many of the design principles that began

with the Arts and Crafts Movement, not only the ideas of Morris but also Americans like Arthur Wesley Dow, are still being taught in design schools (many of which were first set up during the Arts and Crafts Movement). It was in the late 1960s and 1970s (a bad decade by most accounts), that a revival of handcrafts occurred as the much-maligned Baby Boomers began to question the society they had grown up in. Yes, some of the handcrafts were macramé plant hangers in the shape of owls, but much of it wasn't. Craft fairs also arose at that time, and have become a permanent fixture—either weekly, like the Portland Saturday Market in Oregon, or once a year, as part of a festival celebrating a famous local product or event, or to attract people downtown. The American Crafts Council, set up in 1943, began to hold shows in 1966.

ABOVE: The entry hall of the Wilson bungalow was to have been a study in the original plan, and still has the paneling and bookcases (unseen at right) to show for it. A built-in seat with storage has been added, and on the left, a set of French doors open into the living room.

OPPOSITE: My first bungalow in Berkeley was a really standard type that's called a "California bungalow" locally. This differentiates the stucco variety from the wood-sided variety usually called "craftsman bungalow" around these parts. (Craftsman with a capital "C" refers to houses and other things designed or manufactured by Gustav Stickley's company.). It has a Chicago window, an elephantine column, and the prevalent bungalow door with eight beveled lights and a corbeled shelf over a couple of panels below.

◻THE IMPORTANCE◻ OF BEAUTY

THE PLEASURABLE EXERCISE OF OUR ENERGIES IS AT ONCE THE SOURCE OF ALL
ART AND THE CAUSE OF ALL HAPPINESS: THAT IS TO SAY, IT IS THE END OF LIFE.

WILLIAM MORRIS

Having been to design school, I certainly knew about the Arts and Crafts
Movement, and of William Morris's principles. But I don't know that I consciously
applied them to my own life. Instead, some kind of knowing just came from making
things, and from observing my fellow craftspeople. It struck me that a craft often
chooses its practitioner—most of the true craftspeople I know and have known are
almost compelled to make whatever it is they make. And I began to value craft in a way
that I don't think most people do, ever since art was split into "fine" and "applied." I
came to think that crafts were better than "fine art," because they were not only beautiful
but could also be used. (I don't think I was familiar with Morris's famous saying at that
point. For the uninitiated, that would be, "Have nothing in your houses that you do not
know to be useful and believe to be beautiful.") It's not that paintings and prints and

With the exception of the pomegranates, just about everything in this picture shows the hand and thought of a craftsperson for at least part of its manufacture and design, from the leaded glass in the windows, to the joinery of the table and chair, to the hand hammering of the lamp, bowl, and boxes on the table.

sculpture aren't fine things—I just figure that a vase is a sculpture into which you can also put flowers.

Because I made things, I also developed an appreciation for function, quite outside of beauty. Many things that are quite beautiful do not function well, though this is also true of things that are ugly. Both ends of this equation annoy me. A beautiful teapot that dribbles is just as bad as an ugly teapot that pours perfectly; there is no reason why there cannot be a beautiful teapot that pours perfectly. A thing that is both beautiful and functional is, in Morris's words, "a joy to the maker and the user."

Then there are things which are both ugly and don't function well, like the computer I'm writing this on. I'm just not willing to give up the parts that DO function well, that allow me to move words around and rewrite and put in extra sentences in the middle of something. It's merely that everything else about it makes me want to scream . . .

An interesting experiment took place in the early 1990s. Two Japanese researchers decided to test the theory that attractive things worked better. They studied automated teller machines, all with identical functions, system of operation, and number of buttons. They interviewed people who were using them, and found that the machines with the buttons and screens arranged attractively were perceived as being easier to use. A scientist in Israel, seeing their research, figured that it must be because aesthetic preferences are culturally dependent, and Japanese culture is known for its aesthetic tradition. So he performed the same experiment in Israel, Israelis

not being known for their great devotion to beauty, intending to disprove the theory. He got the ATM layouts from Japan, translated them into Hebrew, designed a new experiment with rigorous methodology, and was surprised to find that not only did his experiment confirm the Japanese findings, the correlation was even stronger in Israel than it had been in Japan. I guess it's always good to have scientists quantify what craftspeople already know.

It is generally agreed that the Arts and Crafts Movement planted the seeds of Modernism, or at least prepared the soil for the seeds of Modernism to grow. It's also generally agreed that the bungalow led to the ranch house, and I have to admit they have some things in common. But something I perceive as a terrible thing, a thing that troubles us still, happened in the process. Beauty was removed from the equation. Ornament of any sort was excised. Louis Sullivan's "form follows function" creed was perverted from its original meaning, and the Machine triumphed. Le Corbusier could proclaim, "A house is a machine for living in." That people didn't want to live in machines was eventually made clear, but not before business had realized that lack of ornament was also cheaper. Modernism in the hands of its talented originators was one thing, but unlike bungalows, when it filtered down to the masses it was dreadful. America became a place of boxes—office tower boxes, house boxes, faceless stucco apartment buildings, big box stores, strip malls. Do you know what a vacant retail space is called, one that has been built and dry-walled but not improved for a specific tenant? It's called a "white box." Many of us spend our days working (and, in many cases, living) in white boxes, desperately trying to make them more homey by putting up family photos or personal mementos. We are surrounded by *beige boxes*—computer equipment, file cabinets, and *charcoal boxes*—TV's, stereo equipment. The interior "built environment" around us is mostly spray-textured drywall, laminates, and vinyl floors. The exterior "built environment" is mostly synthetic stucco, cinder blocks, and vinyl windows. We live in a country that has become more and more "placeless."

The Arts and Crafts Movement believed that beauty was important. They believed that beauty and usefulness

OPPOSITE, ABOVE: The Modernists stripped our architecture of ornament, even so much ornament as this simple arch top window with art glass on a Chicago bungalow. Modernist adherents who are the professors in most architecture schools have turned out a generation of architects, most of whom don't understand ornament or what to do with it, because they never learned. Anyone daring to suggest that buildings might be beautiful, rather than "challenging" or "stimulating" or "thought-provoking" or whatever adjective they care to use, would be viewed as hopelessly old-fashioned. Nor should the fact that ornament costs money and clients don't want to pay for it be left out of the equation. Bungalows were built at a time when even the most utilitarian of buildings (warehouses, for instance) or objects (water heaters, for example) were ornamented because it was a matter of pride. It would have been an insult to the community at large to throw up a building that resembled some of the tilt-up concrete buildings we put up with today—and people still cared about the opinion of the larger community.

OPPOSITE, BELOW: The Batchelder "Wisteria" tile on the front of this bedroom fireplace at Artemisia is not only beautiful but also extremely rare.

together were the highest form of human expression. They believed that labor could be pleasurable and even spiritual. They were not against ornamentation—they were against ornament being tacked on at random. They believed that the built environment mattered. They were right, though they were in the minority.

Although there are still sweatshops, factory conditions are better, at least in first world countries, though there is still the distressing practice of merely moving the sweatshops offshore. Certainly the working classes now have far more in the way of material wealth than their nineteenth-century counterparts. We in the Revival are right as well, though we are also in the minority. Maybe that's just the way it is. Even Morris recognized it, saying, "If we could only explain to those thoughtful men, and the millions of whom they are the flower, what the thing is that we love, which is to us as the bread we eat, and the air we breathe, but about which they know nothing and feel nothing, save a vague instinct of repulsion, then the seed of victory might be sown."

My first encounter with the words of John Ruskin was as a child. This quote was framed and hung on the wall of the local Baskin-Robbins ice cream store: "There is nothing in the world that some man cannot make a little worse and sell a little cheaper, and he who considers price only is that man's lawful prey." Well, at least they were being up-front about it. Unfortunately, this is the credo of many businesses, and a great many people consider price only, either because of their financial circumstances, or because they don't care about anything else. The great paradox of the Arts and Crafts Movement is that

ABOVE: I would hope that whoever carved the lion brackets that adorn this Milwaukee Prairie-style house took some pleasure in the work, a sense of pride in a job well done, that maybe he took his children by to show them the finished product and say, "Look, I made this." Or at least for the part of the time when he wasn't thinking, "Geez, I have to carve another damn lion bracket."

OPPOSITE: Anyone who has ever done any finish carpentry knows how hard it is to miter molding that meets at weird angles, like the moldings of this triangular inset in the arched colonnade dividing the living room and dining rooms of a Memphis bungalow. All this red gumwood, carefully finished and fitted, walls carefully plastered, oak floors top nailed, each nail being set below the floor and the holes carefully puttied, all for the benefit of the working people whose first home this was.

well-crafted things cost more, putting them out of reach for the vast majority of people on Earth. A well-crafted thing that *is* affordable is likely the product of a country where wages are low, and quite possibly the result of exploitation of the labor force in that country. A similar paradox exists for the individual craftspeople—a one-of-a-kind object is a joy to the craftsperson who makes it, but likely to be more expensive. Producing objects in larger quantities lowers the price, but turns the craftsperson into a small factory with an assembly line.

But there was one well-crafted thing that did succeed, that working people could afford, and that was the bungalow. Bungalows were what we would now call "affordable housing." But unlike today's affordable housing, which uses the cheapest materials possible, is poorly designed, and looks like hell in about five years (although, admittedly, that's true even of much of today's "market-rate" housing), bungalows were built with old-growth timber, real plaster, wooden windows and doors, wood floors, and built-ins, which are now found only in very high-end houses. And they were actually affordable to regular people.

In some ways the revival HAS succeeded, even as the original movement did. Arts and Crafts has become popular as a style, and people are waking up to the charms of bungalows and other Arts and Crafts houses. In popular culture, of course, the philosophy has been left out. Real success will come if we find a way to solve the paradox and make the philosophy known. One thing I think we could do is to wrest the word "craft" back into respectability. Here are two definitions of *craft* from the dictionary:

craft: (noun) an occupation, trade, or pursuit requiring manual dexterity or
the application of artistic skill.
craft: (verb) to make or produce with care, skill, or ingenuity.

Maybe we need to come up with a different name for the Arts and Crafts Movement. Most people think "arts and crafts" means making things out of Popsicle sticks or using puff paint to put cutesy designs on sweatshirts. Recently the California College of Arts and Crafts, founded in 1907 here in Oakland, changed its name to the California College of the Arts. Similarly, the American Craft Museum in New York changed its name to the Museum of Arts and Design. The reasons cited by both institutions were that the lines between craft, design, and fine art have become blurred, even mentioning that as a goal of the original Arts and Crafts Movement. If you believe that, I have a bridge to sell you. Craft has merely been excised, made invisible. They gave up the battle to bring the term back to respectability, leaving it to the purveyors of cuteness, the fabric stores and craft emporiums. That doesn't mean the battle can't be won. It's true the odds aren't very good, but I have always subscribed to the words of Margaret Mead, "Never doubt that a small group of thoughtful, committed citizens can change the world. Indeed, it's the only thing that ever has."

> MOST PEOPLE THINK "ARTS AND CRAFTS" MEANS MAKING THINGS OUT OF POPSICLE STICKS OR USING PUFF PAINT TO PUT CUTESY DESIGNS ON SWEATSHIRTS.

For myself, I have my own paradox. Rather at odds with my Arts and Crafts beliefs is my great love for kitsch and all things tacky. Maybe a love of beauty just has to be balanced with a love of the surpassingly hideous—I don't know. Maybe it's like the Zen koan—not actually solvable. But I have come up with my own theory regarding art, architecture, and design, which somehow, if not actually resolving the paradox, at least gives me a structure which allows for all sides of it. My theory, which I have, and which is mine, and has nothing to do with the brontosaurus, is as follows:

Everything must be either beautiful or amusing.

Really exceptional things can actually be both at once. Thus, a really zany bungalow can be both beautiful and amusing. Following this theory, I can value a beautiful bungalow as well as a Googie coffee shop. I can cherish an Arts and Crafts woodblock print and I can also cherish my really hideous bath rug that features two French poodles, the Eiffel Tower, and the phrase "Do Your Own Thing." I can be amused by bungalows whose "expressed structure" is all fake, and I can be amused by Las Vegas. I have tried to apply this to my books as well, and to make them useful and beautiful as well as amusing. I think it's why I like Zen—it's both serious and humorous. I shall end with my favorite Zen joke:

Q. What did the Buddhist say to the hot dog vendor?
A. Make me one with everything.

> I CAN CHERISH AN ARTS AND CRAFTS WOODBLOCK PRINT AND I CAN ALSO CHERISH MY REALLY HIDEOUS BATH RUG THAT FEATURES TWO FRENCH POODLES, THE EIFFEL TOWER, AND THE PHRASE "DO YOUR OWN THING."

In the classical orders, the gable on this Memphis bungalow would be called a broken pediment, and it even has
a "keystone" in the center of the shallow arch of the porch
entablature, though the whole thing is made of wood. The
pillars are square but their recessed panels also make them
look vaguely classical. But then there are three beam ends
sticking out of the gable, and wide enclosed eaves from
the Prairie style. This would all be amusing enough, but
then this whole construct is sitting on top of two of the
biggest honkin' piers I've ever seen, complete with arches.
It's the architectural equivalent of those guys you see in
the West wearing a silver belt buckle the size of
a dinner plate.

□ BIBLIOGRAPHY □

Doing research on the Web is like using a library assembled piecemeal by pack rats and vandalized nightly.

Roger Ebert

King, Anthony D. *The Bungalow: The production of a global culture.* London, England: Routledge and Kegan Paul plc, 1984.

Morgan. *Building with Assurance.* Chicago, Illinois: Morgan Woodwork Organization, 1921.

Wilson, Henry L. *A Short Sketch of the Evolution of the Bungalow: From Its Primitive Crudeness to Its Present State of Artistic Beauty and Cozy Convenience.* Los Angeles, California. n.d. Reprint by Dover Publications, Mineola, New York, 1993.

Duchscherer, Paul and Keister, Douglas. *The Bungalow: America's Arts and Crafts Home.* New York, New York: Penguin Books, 1995.

Duchscherer, Paul and Keister, Douglas. *Outside the Bungalow: America's Arts and Crafts Garden.* New York, New York: Penguin Books, 1999.

Parry, Linda. *William Morris.* London, England: Phillip Wilson Publishers in Association with the Victoria and Albert Museum, 1996.

Wilhide, Elizabeth. *William Morris: Décor and Design.* London, England: Pavilion Books Limited, 1991.

Smith, Bruce, and Vertikoff, Alexander. *Greene and Greene Masterworks.* San Francisco, California: Chronicle Books, 1998.

Makinson, Randell L. *Greene and Greene: The Passion and the Legacy.* Salt Lake City, Utah: Gibbs Smith, Publisher, 1998.

Pfeiffer, Bruce Brooks. *Frank Lloyd Wright: Selected Houses.* Tokyo, Japan: A.D.A. EDITA Tokyo Company, Ltd, 1991.

Norman, Donald A. *Emotional Design: Why We Love (Or Hate) Everyday Things.* New York, New York: Basic Books, 2004.

Sears Roebuck and Company. *Honor-bilt Modern Homes.* Chicago, Illinois: 1926. Reprint by Dover Publications, Mineola, New York, 1991.

Ray H. Bennett Lumber Company. *Bennett Homes: Better-Built Ready-Cut.* North Tonawanda, New York, 1920. Reprint by Dover Publications, Mineola, New York, 1993.

The Aladdin Company. *Aladdin Homes: "Built in a Day" Catalog #29.* Bay City, Michigan, 1917. Reprint by Dover Publications, Mineola, New York, 1995.

Gordon-Van Tine Company. *Gordon-Van-Tine Homes.* Davenport, Iowa, 1923. Reprint by Dover Publications, Mineola, New York, 1992.

The Building Brick Association of America. *One Hundred Bungalows.* Boston, Massachusetts: 1912. Reprint by Dover Publications, Mineola, New York, 1994.

Loizeaux Lumber Company. *Loizeaux's Plan Book #7.* Plainfield, New Jersey, 1927. Reprint by Dover Publications, Mineola, New York, 1992.

Winter, Robert. *The California Bungalow.* Los Angeles, California: Hennessey and Ingalls, Inc., 1980.

Stickley, Gustav. *Craftsman Homes.* New York, New York: Craftsman Publishing Company, 1909. Reprint by Dover Publications, Mineola, New York, 1979.

Stickley, Gustav. *More Craftsman Homes.* New York, New York: Craftsman Publishing Company, 1912. Reprint by Dover Publications, Mineola, New York, 1982.

Radford, William A. *Radford's Artistic Bungalows.* Chicago, Illinois: Radford Architectural Company, 1908. Reprint by Dover Publications, Mineola, New York, 1997.

Hodgson, Fred T. *Practical Bungalow and Cottages for Town and Country.* Chicago, Illinois: Frederick J. Drake and Company, 1906.

Lancaster, Clay. *The American Bungalow.* New York, New York: Abbeville Press, 1985. Reprint by Dover Publications, Mineola, New York, 1995.

Prentice, Helaine Kaplan and Blair, and City of Oakland Planning Department. *Rehab Right.* Oakland, California: City of Oakland, 1978. Reprint by Ten Speed Press, Berkeley, California, 1986.

Lewis Manufacturing Company. *Lewis Homes: Homes of Character.* Bay City, Michigan, 1923.

Keith, M. L. *Keith's Magazine on Home Building, July 1918.* Minneapolis, Minnesota.

WEB ARTICLES:

Morris, William. "The Lesser Arts of Life." An Address Delivered in Support of the Society for the Protection of Ancient Buildings. London, 1882. http://www.burrows.com/morris/lesser.html

Faragher, John Mack. "Bungalow and Ranch House: The Architectural Backwash of California." *Western Historical Quarterly* Summer 2001. http://www.historycooperative.org/journals/whq/32.2/faragher.htm

Phillips, Kerry. "What is a Bungalow?" Sacramento Bungalow Heritage Association, 2003. http://www.sacbungalow.org/whabunga.htm

Morris, William. The William Morris Internet Archive. http://www.marxists.org/archive/morris/index.htm

□BUNG

THE ULTiMATE ART